MY LIFE AS A GIRL
REVOLUTIONARY

RED STAR TATTOO

SONJA LARSEN

RANDOM HOUSE CANADA

PUBLISHED BY RANDOM HOUSE CANADA

Copyright © 2016 Sonja Larsen

Published in 2016 by Random House Canada, a division of Penguin Random House Canada Limited. Distributed in Canada by Penguin Random House Canada Limited, Toronto.

www.penguinrandomhouse.ca

Library and Archives Canada Cataloguing in Publication

Larsen, Sonja (Sonja A.), author
Red star tattoo : my life as a girl revolutionary / Sonja Larsen.

Issued in print and electronic formats.

ISBN 978-0-345-81527-9
eBook ISBN 978-0-345-81529-3

1. Larsen, Sonja (Sonja A.). 2. Women revolutionaries—United States—Biography. 3. Women communists—United States—Biography. 4. Radicalism—United States. I. Title.

HX843.7.L37A3 2016   335'.83092   C2015-905462-1

Book design by Terri Nimmo

Cover photograph courtesy of the author

Photograph on page 242 by Ann Marie Martin.
All other photographs courtesy of the author.

Printed and bound in the United States of America

2   4   6   8   9   7   5   3   1

Penguin
Random House
RANDOM HOUSE CANADA

*For Dana & the girls we were
and to Patricia and the women we became*

PART ONE

History is moving in zig-zags and
by roundabout ways.

VLADIMIR LENIN

ONE

A canvas backpack.

A sleeping bag.

A drinking cup that collapsed flat into a little case.

Two matching wooden bowls, one for Dale and one for me.

A combination fork and spoon. The spork.

My teddy bear.

Some clothes.

A toothbrush.

A small case, hand embroidered by my mother, to hold my "travelling papers."

Pounds and pounds of homemade granola, made the night before and packed in plastic bags. Slightly burned.

I remember what we packed for the journey.

But what did my parents say to me when it was time to go—goodbye? See you soon? See you later?

When the drivers slowed down to look at us, I tried to catch their eye. Sometimes I wiggled my outstretched thumb slightly, optimistically, and sometimes I tried to look sad and hopeful. Anything to imprint this scene in their mind: little girl sitting on a grey canvas backpack, young man with a guitar case, standing by the highway. Anything to slow them down until curiosity or sympathy made them stop.

Everyone knew that a kid was better than a dog or a woman for hitchhiking. At the Sweetgrass commune, where me and Dale, my parents, and another dozen or so people lived, everyone pitched in, did their share to keep things going. This was something I could do. I was eight years old and already an experienced hitchhiker, a travelling partner for anyone who needed luck and company on the road. I'd also sung in the Sweetgrass band that played folk and gospel songs at old folks' homes and rock and roll at high school dances. I'd helped sell wildflowers, daisies and goldenrod and fireweed tied up in twine, to tourists in the city. But hitchhiking was the thing I did best. Up and down country roads into town, or the hundred-mile trip from Lennoxville to Montreal and back.

I was Dale's plan to get west cheap and in a hurry. Dale was in his early twenties and from Los Angeles. He and another Californian played the lead guitars in the band. They'd helped start Sweetgrass, but Quebec winters and the winding down of the Vietnam War had them longing for home. His friend had already left with another commune member who was caught up in a custody battle for her baby. Dale and I were the second wave. My parents and a few others would be following soon. Behind us was Sweetgrass. Ahead of us was California and a new life. But in between was this long stretch of road.

By day three I could feel Dale starting to wonder if this highway was more than my small charm could manage. We'd spent hours waiting to catch the next ride. I knew it didn't help to look too miserable or be crying. No one wanted to deal with that kind of kid. Instead I sat by the side of the road with my teddy bear and sucked my thumb, trying to look younger and cuter than I really was.

To keep us entertained, Dale played his guitar and sang. He sang the Beatles and Dylan but the old country songs were my favourites.

Take me home, my heart is heavy and my feet are sore
Take me home, I don't wanna roam no more

I liked that song, I liked the idea that what we were doing was roaming, and that when we got to California our roaming days would be over.

I watched our stuff while Dale went into the truck stop across the way to get us some soup and crackers. It was getting dark and starting to rain. Through the bright restaurant windows I watched Dale talking to someone at the counter. They both turned around and Dale pointed at me, across the road. I waved. Probably I had the teddy bear out, too, since I used him both as a pillow and a plea. When Dale came out he told me the man at the truck stop lived just down the road. We could spend the night if we wanted, get cleaned up. His wife was expecting us.

There was just one problem: he was on a motorcycle, so he could only take one of us at a time.

"Don't be scared," the man said to me. I don't know if it was the rumble of the motorcycle, the wheels beginning to roll, or the word, *scared*, that made the bottom of my feet tingle, that gave me that just-about-to-fall feeling, as we sped away from Dale and the parking lot, and onto the dark road.

Before the commune my parents used to read to me almost every night. We read *Winnie-the-Pooh*, Grimms' fairy tales, all of the Narnia Chronicles. There was a time when I believed my parents' ability to pull meaning from tiny black lines on a page was its own kind of magic. For the first time I could see that I might be in a story too, the girl who went down the rabbit hole or disappeared through a secret door. As the motorcycle curved in the drizzling dark, I sat on the seat in front of the man, enclosed by his arms, breathing in the smells of his leather jacket, and the wet trees, and the old-penny smell of rain hitting the pavement.

When we got to the man's house, his wife was waiting out front, her body a dark silhouette in the doorway. While the man rode back to pick up Dale, his wife helped me get ready for bed. She asked if I had a prayer I said before bedtime and when I said no, she taught me one she said every child should know.

Now I lay me down to sleep,
I pray the Lord my soul to keep;
If I die before I wake,
I pray the Lord my soul to take.

I knew there was no God. When I was six or seven our family dog died. My parents and sister and I had just moved to Montreal and a girl on our street told me that if I prayed to God for ten days, my dog would come back. We had never discussed God in our home, but I thought maybe he was something new, the way Canada was new, and French was new. When the dog didn't come back I asked my parents about God. *He's not real,* they said. *He's just a story people tell to make themselves feel better.* And what about Santa Claus? *Same thing.*

We didn't have a lot of stories to make us feel better except maybe that we were the kind of people that didn't need them. Later I would learn that Bud, my mother's father, and his father before him, had been Texas-born preachers for the Church of the Nazarene. The women weren't supposed to wear makeup and no one was supposed to dance. My mother was born on an Indian reservation where Bud was stationed at a mission and as a child she'd moved a lot. Minnesota, Maryland, Washington. Over ten states by the time she was sixteen. But by the time I came along not even

Bud was a believer anymore. He gave up his calling but not before telling my aunt she was a slut when she was raped, not before making my pregnant sixteen-year-old mother get married outside of town so it wouldn't be listed in their local paper. Not before the damage was done.

That first marriage barely lasted two years and was over when her husband started to hit her. There was no one serious after that until she met my father at a dance hall. He was smart and funny and a good dancer. He loved books like she did. He played guitar. He had a college degree. But even so, my mother didn't want to get married because she didn't want her daughter, Patti, to have a different last name than she did. When my dad said he'd adopt Patti, my mother said yes. In the photos they stand together, all of them smiling. And nine months later I was born.

My mother was sick with kidney problems during the pregnancy and when I was slow to sit up as a baby they worried something was wrong with me. "But you were just lazy," my sister said. "You just liked being held." "You were a very loved baby," my mother said. She thought love was like the fluoride in the water of my baby formula, that it protected me to the bones.

Milwaukee was the town where the fluoride was in the water, the place where my father grew up in a working-class neighbourhood in a house his parents bought before he was born. It's where I was born, and a place my mother loved and admired until the race riots of 1967, when a black friend of my mother's stayed with us for two days because it was not safe for her to be on the streets. We left Milwaukee the same year.

Hawaii was where we went next, first on one island and then another for my father's teaching job. It was where we stole pineapples from a field and ate them until our mouths were raw waiting for his first paycheque to come in. My dad claimed that when I was two or three, I could predict the suit of cards before he turned them over. So that would have been in Hawaii too. I had mixed feelings about that story. Sometimes it made me

feel special, and other times it made me feel like I would never be special again. Hawaii was where we'd bought the family dog by the side of the road from a man we suspected was selling him for meat. We named him Aso, Tagalog for dog. It's where I loved the ocean until one day a wave knocked me over and I didn't love it anymore. Hawaii is where we left one summer for a visit to the mainland and never went back.

We moved to Montreal after that, a whole new country, away from the Vietnam War. It was a place for a fresh start, a haven not just for draft dodgers but other disillusioned Americans as well. My father wanted to write a novel. My mother wanted to go back to school. They had big plans, plans to be happy. In Montreal I learned about God and the different words there were for each thing, how you could think you knew something—how to ask the time or how to say hello—and then go someplace where it turned out maybe you didn't know anything at all.

Montreal was where the dog died and we got a new dog and moved to the east end of the city where we lived above a used car dealer. My father took me out in a purple snowsuit and taught me one of the few French words he knew: *neige*. Another word was *bonjour,* which we used on the neighbour kids as we made snowmen and snow angels in the vacant lot beside our apartment. My sister and I were the only English kids on our block and also the only ones to have pets, allowances or rooms of our own. At the corner store I bought the other kids candy and they taught me the names of each one: *gomme balloune, sucette, réglisse.*

It was harder for my teenage sister. Once again she was the new kid. In Hawaii she'd been the only white kid in her school, now she was the only English kid on the block, caught between worlds. Once she did make some friends she got picked up by the cops and harassed for being out past the government-imposed curfew. We'd only been in Quebec a year before the FLQ crisis had broken out. There had been kidnappings of politicians, a murder. All around the city separatists were spraying graffiti on the walls and blowing up mailboxes in the rich English-speaking neighbourhoods.

Patti was tired of moving and probably tired of taking care of me too. Every day after school before my parents came home from work she babysat me and we watched *Dark Shadows* together although my mother said TV rotted your brain. My sister was furious when I told my mother what we'd been doing, but I thought my mother would want to know the truth, that TV wasn't so bad and our brains were just fine. Instead she took the power cord away.

When my parents fought Patti would bring me into her room and turn up her radio. It was always my sister and me together, even if she was mad at me. But when she fought with my parents, I didn't know what to do or where to go.

My parents had come so far but so much was still the same. Canada wasn't what they had imagined. Here, as in the States, there was injustice, deep divides between people and, it turned out, between each other. My parents weren't happy. My sister wasn't happy. Maybe I wasn't happy either, but I just didn't know it.

When my parents weren't fighting they were trying to make up. They took long walks, explored the city. They were shocked to find taverns where women weren't allowed, and pleasantly surprised at how easy it was to find marijuana and hash. One night the bamboo blinds in the living room caught fire when they went out and left a candle burning. My sister called the fire department and kept me calm until they arrived. Another day she took me to the hospital for stitches when I fell down in the gravel parking lot beside our apartment while my parents were still at work.

We found a nicer neighbourhood and a better apartment. Our parents made new friends. At dinner parties they debated about Marxism and feminism but at home that only added fuel to their arguments, their dissatisfaction with each other and with themselves. When I was older my mother told me she'd spent hours at her job thinking up ways to kill herself so that it would look like an accident. A car crash, a fall, a death by drowning. It was her first job with life insurance.

I went to an English school down the street. In my old neighbourhood I'd been *la petite Américaine,* a novelty because of my language and my weekly allowance. Here I was no longer the only kid with my own room or pocket money and there were all kinds of English I had not even known about—Jewish, Greek, Italian—but I was none of them. They didn't know what to make of me. I had to be something—a nationality, a religion—but I was nothing, an American mutt. The girls at my school chanted, *Sonja, Sonja, don't be blue, Frankenstein was ugly too!* and this seemed almost harder to understand than a new language. Not words substituted for other words, but words that seemed to mean one thing but really meant another.

My parents kept fighting. One night my mother came into my room and woke me up to ask me if I thought she should divorce my father. Patti ran in, shouting at her to leave us alone. Patti was fifteen then, the same age my mother was when she'd gotten pregnant. They even had the same name—my mom was

13

Big Patti and my sister was Little Patti. But looking up at them now as they stood face to face screaming I could see that they were the same size.

Around that time my mother and I went to visit a friend they'd met at the dinner parties. Debby had just moved with her baby to a commune called Sweetgrass, a hundred miles outside of Montreal. That weekend, nobody shouted or cried. Instead they sang and played music.

I didn't want to leave. I wanted to play tambourine and learn how to sing harmony. Maybe it was only supposed to have been for a few weeks, or a month. Maybe if I had known that would be the end of my family, I would not have asked to stay. Maybe. All I knew was that I wanted out. Out of my new school. Out of the yelling and fighting at home, away from slammed doors and tears. I don't remember asking to leave my family, I just remember asking to stay at Sweetgrass. When I told Debby I wanted to live there, she said I had to ask the group, which I did at dinner one night. Nobody said no.

I spent my days exploring the barn, hanging out with Debby and her baby. A few weeks later my mother decided to move to Sweetgrass too. My father and sister stayed in the city. My mother started to learn the banjo and the first song she learned was about Jesse James. She decided to change her name to Jesse, since there was already a Patti at Sweetgrass too. From then on that's who she was to me. Not Mommy or Pat or Patti, but Jesse.

The peaceful atmosphere didn't last; not long after we arrived the commune started fighting too. I felt like our unhappiness was contagious, or maybe that it just took time to see what tensions were already there, like eyes adjusting to a change in light. I could not help but notice the love affairs and power struggles, and in both some people were content with the way things were and others wanted more. Maybe the Americans had been waiting out the draft or maybe they just wanted to go home, but it wasn't hard to sell some people on joining them in the dream of a proper farm in a place where it was always warm and we could really live off the land. Debby had a custody battle she was running from. Half a dozen decided to go to Northern California, and half a dozen stayed behind. I must have wanted to go, because once again I was among the first to leave. My mother, and even my father, would follow later.

But not Patti. She was too old to believe them anymore when they said it was going to be different someplace else. She didn't want to live on a commune or move three thousand miles. Usually she was the one to storm out of the room but after my parents could not convince her to go they signed papers to make her an emancipated minor and left for California without her. She was fifteen years old.

15

I was already on the road with Dale by then. I remember packing the granola, my travelling papers, the teddy bear. Had he been my favourite toy before he was my only one? I remember that I liked his short stubby body and long arms, the feel of his fur and how he looked like the pictures in my *Winnie-the-Pooh* book. I'd had him since I was one so he'd been to Milwaukee, Hawaii, places I could barely recall. He'd been everywhere with me. By the side of the road, on the motorcycle, tucked into a bed that smelled of soap, keeping me company as I learned prayers I didn't believe.

The Englishman in the funny-looking car picked us up on day six or seven after we'd made it across the prairies, sometimes sleeping beside the road. We got in his car in the morning and by afternoon, he'd decided what we really needed was a cookout. That's what he called it. With camping and hot dogs and roasted marshmallows on the campfire.

He was touring Canada. "Big country," he said. We were in the Rockies by then, finally closer to where we were going than where we'd been.

We drove to a supermarket to buy what we needed. I didn't like marshmallows, but the Englishman refused to believe this.

"All children love sweets," he said.

I'd never been inside such a large supermarket before. Underneath the bright lights with the soft music playing in the background, the name of the store echoed in my head. *Safeway.* There was every kind of marshmallow. Big dusty white, and tiny pastel pink and green, all puffed inside their plastic bags. The Englishman said we had to try them all.

At the campsite, I looked for sticks that were the size and width the man told me to find and he cut little points on each branch with a penknife to put the marshmallows on. The mini marshmallows burned into tiny lumps of charred sweetness. The coloured ones dripped from the burning wood like melted plastic. I ate them burnt and lightly toasted and everywhere in between. Dale wouldn't eat the hot dogs or the marshmallows but the Englishman didn't even notice.

He had a lot of enamel and metal pins, all in a little suitcase, stuck onto cloth. Some were souvenirs from places he'd visited and others were military wings and stars. He told me he'd been an air force pilot. He said he'd once shot down a Russian spy plane "in an area where to this very day the Russians deny ever being." He showed me a pin he'd taken off the uniform of the dead pilot. He said that information was "absolutely top secret." I nodded seriously, but I knew I was going to tell someone someday. He gave me a little yellow smiley-face button to pin on my backpack.

17

I ate the marshmallows, I listened to his stories. Finally I pretended I was sleepy, and crouched down into my sleeping bag. In the dark, I could smell the woodsmoke and my own sugary breath. The trees in the campground were as tall as buildings.

The next morning the Englishman offered to drive us all the way to California but Dale decided to stick with the original plan, which was for us to take the Greyhound bus from Vancouver and down through Washington, where hitchhiking was illegal. I was glad; the Englishman's sweet tooth and the thought of him taking the pin off a dead man made me feel queasy, like a road with too many turns.

At the border the guard looked through Dale's pack and in his guitar. When he got to me the guard took out all my clothes from the pack and I had a sudden fear that he'd cut open Pooh Bear. Instead he carefully felt the bear's body and paws. Then he let us get back on the bus.

I loved the bus. On the bus I didn't have to worry about feeling sick or how soon I might need to pee, since there was a toilet in the back. I sat up to the window on my knees, my forehead touching the cool glass, watching for evidence of California, in the grass or the trees or the houses. The green tinted windows made everything look like a Kodachrome picture. The ripple of water, a mailbox by the side of the road, an old woman's face in a passing car—they could all be photographs, postcards.

But what I loved most about the bus was the way we rolled by, invisible to the world, instead of standing on the side of the road, holding a piece of cardboard that said *West*. What I loved best was that when we went by, people didn't know I was even there. They didn't want to feed me candy or teach me prayers. They looked right at me but all they saw was their own reflection in the moving glass.

TWO

Our California rendezvous point with the other commune members was the Oakland House, an old Victorian mansion in West Oakland. It was home to at least a dozen people already, including a theatre collective. By the time Dale and I got there some of the others from Quebec had already arrived: Debby, Dale's friend Casey, another American. More people trickled in every week. There were also other kids: Debby's baby and two older children, Ben and Molly, siblings who had just moved from Berkeley with their dad.

California was supposed to be the land of sunshine

but my first impression was the cool, shadowy darkness inside the Oakland House. When one of Molly's hamsters went missing we went through every room and discovered the dumbwaiter shaft and the crawl space between the floors. The house was full of hiding spots for lost animals. We spent days looking although we knew the hamster must have died.

When we weren't exploring we were in the kitchen with Debby and her baby. Debby fed us soup and toast and oatmeal and sometimes even took us to a park where I saw the ocean. But mostly we stayed inside. At the Oakland House there was only one rule: don't go outside alone. Outside was burnt-out cars and danger, outside was where Ben had seen a man get shot. But inside there were no rules. There were always new people to meet, rooms to explore, a ballroom and microphones and speakers that could fill it with sound.

The ballroom was where we gathered the night of the party, the night that everyone, even the grownups, played hide-and-go-seek. The darkness was supposed to heighten our senses. So was the acid. The acid was on tiny bits of coloured paper. I didn't take any acid but the older kids did: quarter hits, baby hits, while the thirty or so adults had bigger doses. Were my parents there yet? I don't think so.

We'd been waiting all evening for the right moment, a moment called "peaking," to turn off the lights and start the game, but the darkness was still a surprise, a

21

breathing whispering giggling surprise. There were sounds you could hear only in the dark. In the light you never heard breathing or footsteps or the sound of clothes moving on a person's body. The object of the game was to reach home base without getting found or tagged. Home base was a lighting tower on wheels that kept getting moved around. Hide-and-go-seek evolved into king of the castle, with players attacking and defending the tower with cardboard-tube swords. Somehow my lip got split and for the rest of the night I was a monster chasing people and roaring my way through the Oakland House's many rooms. The darkness, the sound of my voice in my ears, the salty warm taste of blood in my mouth. How long did we live at the Oakland House? Days, weeks, maybe months? It was easy to lose track of time.

From the Oakland House we moved north to our new commune, 180 acres at the northern edge of the Sacramento Valley. My parents had both arrived and each found new lovers on the commune. My father's new girlfriend was a woman from the Quebec commune and my mother's boyfriend, Karl, was a tall, quiet young man who had come from the Oakland House. He was one of a half dozen or so people, including Molly and Ben and their dad, who had all joined our vision of living off the land. The two-storey farmhouse couldn't hold us all and so we slept wherever we could: in the house, in a small outbuilding, in the barn, and even in an old broken cube van. I'd share rooms with the other kids or my mother, and for a while I had a bed in a hallway on the second floor.

We called our new home Live Oak Farm but even the kids at my school knew that we wouldn't be able to have a real farm there. We were off the waterline for one thing, and in the middle of a drought for another. Besides which, it was ranch country, all around us was star thistle and oak, a landscape all the shades of a rattlesnake.

Still, we dug the dirt, we planted the seeds. We managed to grow zucchinis the size of watermelons. "You don't see *these* in the supermarket," someone said. For good reason as it turned out, since our enormous produce tasted woody and bitter. It couldn't be sold and could barely be eaten. But we did eat it, at nearly every meal. We grew a field of beans but never quite figured out how to get the rocks out of the crop. We spread blood from the nearby cattle yard to fertilize the ground, but it killed everything we'd planted. The smell of blood in the dry heat was nauseating, but I couldn't stay away from the ground where new shoots came up radiant green against the stinking

23

black dirt. I could see even then that there were people who could only learn things the hard way. People like us.

We'd bought a two-ton truck to haul our expected future bounty of vegetables to market and after the garden failed we cut down trees and sold firewood door to door and sometimes even used the truck to drive the kids to school when we missed the bus and the other car was broken. The truck barely fit into the school parking lot.

The adults hadn't even wanted to send us to school but after the truancy officer drove out to visit, we had to go. I had no friends except Molly and Ben, but I liked the library and the school lunch, which was a change from the zucchini, beans, and rice we ate every day at the farm.

We often went for days at a time without toilet paper, coffee, tobacco, soap. The adults tried grinding acorns as a coffee substitute and smoking hand-rolled cigarettes made with dried sage leaves. One of the women got caught at the Lucky Supermarket stealing toilet paper and tampons. She tried to hide them under her long skirt. "You don't understand" she said, bursting into tears. "I really need this." The manager was so mortified he let her go.

We were poor but always full of big ideas. Someone borrowed money to buy a backhoe to dig irrigation trenches and I gave up the Christmas money I got

BCPL Checkout

Call number: 332.63085 Lar
Author: Larsen, Soulja
Title: Red star tattoo : my
life as a girl revolutionary
(Soulja A)
Due Date: 24 September
2020 23:59

Call number: 248.843 Hol
Author: Hollis, Rachel (Evangel
planner)
Title: Girl, wash your face
up set for believing the
Due Date: 24 September
2020 23:59

Total checkouts for session:
2
Total checkouts: 13

Total value to check out
items: $60.50

Thank you for returning
items
in the bookdrop
Library processing.ou e

BCPL checkout

Call number: 335.83092 Lar
Author: Larsen, Sonja
(Sonja A.),
Title: Red star tattoo : my
life as a girl revolutionary
Due Date: 24 September
2020 23:59

Call number: 248.843 Hol
Author: Hollis, Rachel (Event
planner)
Title: Girl, wash your face :
stop believing the lies ab
Due Date: 24 September
2020 23:59

Total checkouts for session:
2
Total checkouts:13

Total value of checked out
items: $60.50

Thank you for returning
items
in the bookdrop.
library.brucecounty.on.ca

from my grandparents to help buy gas for it. The men spent a few days with it, out in the field, practising until it broke or they got bored. From a distance the backhoe looked like a sad yellow dinosaur standing beside its nest. After a few months, it got sold and only the hole was left behind.

My other Christmas present that year had a serious worried face and a loud hungry cry. I named the little lamb Bert, after the *Sesame Street* character. A lamb for me, baby goats for Molly and a piglet for Ben. Bert was so small he wasn't even weaned yet. I mixed formula in a bottle, and wondered at Bert's strength, the way he jerked his head on his wobbly little legs to pull the milk from the bottle and how quickly he learned to recognize me from all other humans, bleating and following after me.

"Didn't you even get any clothes for Christmas?" one of the girls in my school asked after the holidays.

"Obviously not," another one said.

No new clothes. But Bert the lamb. And for my birthday in March an old pocket knife and nine paper matches on my carob birthday cake. Later on that spring, there were presents for all the kids: a homemade balance beam, a Shetland stallion named Hacksaw and a second-hand trampoline.

The balance beam was not entirely straight, and it splintered our bare feet. Patti C said the balance beam was like a horse; you always had to get back up after

25

you fell. She taught us all how to point our toes as we walked, how to not look down at the rail.

This Patti was one of the founders of our old commune in Quebec. She had ideas about everything—but especially about children. She had me sucking on buttons to help correct my crooked teeth. It bothered her that I was a mouth-breather so she gave me exercises, *in through the nose, out through the mouth*, to help me learn how to breathe properly. Still, she had trouble fixing herself. She sometimes wore woollen gloves, even in the summer because she had a circulation disease, and she was supposed to quit smoking but she couldn't.

The Shetland pony was Patti C's idea too. But Hacksaw was like the truck and the backhoe and just about everything else we'd done: a mistake. He ran across the field at top speed towards any low-lying branch the minute we got on his back. We hung on as best we could since we didn't own a saddle. When he was not trying to scrape us off his back, he was biting or kicking and when he was not doing that he was trying to jump the fence to get at the neighbour's mare.

The neighbour said he'd shoot the pony dead before he let it mount his horse. I thought Hacksaw would probably do it anyway, even if he could have

understood the risk. That's what sex was, it seemed—
something that made you tear your skin on barbed
wire or forget everything else in the world. I had seen
it with my own eyes, not just in the pony but in the
people at the farm. I had once walked in on Patti C
and Dale and she asked if I wanted to stay and watch.
I said no. Sex was like a scary movie with just the
monster part. I had seen my mother, too, under the
moonlight during a camping trip with her boyfriend
Karl, like strange animals inside their familiar bodies.

Sex made everyone crazy, not just Hacksaw. Even
inside me there was a magnet that drew men in, though
I couldn't feel it, couldn't see it. Sex was the creepy-
crawly feeling of Karl's hand on my thigh a few months
later, like a wasp that could not stay away from fruit.
And just like I did with wasps, I held my breath and
hoped he would go away. Sex was an instinct, not good
or bad, the grown-ups said. Silence was an instinct too.

Maybe people could not help themselves, maybe
they were like dogs that gnawed through doors and
roosters that woke with the sun and rams that battered
themselves senseless. Like Hacksaw, who we finally
gave away before he got himself killed.

But the trampoline—that was not like the backhoe
or the balance beam or the pony. The trampoline was
not a mistake.

The trampoline sat outside the front door of the
house, where steps and a porch should have been.

27

What did we trade, or give up or do without, for this? From the road, you could see us, children and adults, jumping, up and down, some of us more daring than others, our bodies flipping and turning in the air.

At school a popular recess activity was to invent stories that began with "the bad news is . . ."

The bad news is your plane is crashing.

After the bad news is the good news.

The good news is there's a parachute.

The trampoline was pleasure mixed with the familiar pins-and-needles feeling of fear at the very bottoms of my feet. The fear of bouncing too high, of never coming back down, or coming down in the wrong place. But I loved the breeze that my body created as I move up and down, and the way this was close as I could ever come to being weightless.

The bad news was it happened again.

The good news was it wouldn't anymore. Because now I knew. Not to go to my mother's bed if I had a bad dream, and not to get left alone with him. Now I knew.

Every time I got on the trampoline, I played this game in some variation, the good news and the bad news wrapped inside every muscle of my body, the ones that pushed me higher, and the ones that braced me as I came down.

The good news was that after a year of living alone in Montreal my sister had come to California.

The bad news was everyone else was leaving because the commune was falling apart.

Some people, like my father, gave up on the commune and others formed a plan to send a group of people to work in Los Angeles and send the money back to the farm. But after a while it became clear they weren't coming back either. The phone got cut off and my sixteen-year-old sister spent three days in a local jail, picked up for underage hitchhiking until finally the sheriff drove out to let my mother know.

My father wrote from Montreal:

> Hello and how are you? From what I can gather, it
> looks as if you'll have to leave the farm in the near
> future. It's not unexpected, but I suppose it'll be quite a
> shock, I don't know what plans you have made, or if
> you've even started to make them. You know, of course,
> that you could stay with me for as long as you wish.
> You could also visit my parents in Milwaukee (they'd
> be thrilled) stay with your mother or (probably) do
> something with somebody in Seattle. It must be amaz-
> ing to be nine years old and have so many options.

29

So many options, so many choices. I could live any-where I wanted. But it was another story for Bert. There was only one place for him to go.

I was running down Hooker Creek Road with Bert, running just as fast as we could go, but it took my mother and Karl only seconds to catch up to us in his big white van.

It was pure reflex, running—it was the smallest and most useless of gestures. Even as I did it I knew that if I'd really wanted to save Bert, I could have seen this coming, I could have left with him in the middle of the night, instead of bolting down the road at a dead run in broad daylight. Bert, who kept pinning me to the wall, charging me in the yard, knocking me flat, Bert who was teaching me the hard way that I was his whole world, Bert, another mistake. It was too late anyway. The butcher was on his way.

Maybe I thought I owed it to Bert, to love him enough to make his body useful. Maybe I was angry at him, for letting this happen to him. Or I was just hungry. Just tired of lentils and beans. Maybe I said no the first few times. But I know that one day someone made mutton and rice stew, and I said yes.

My sister wouldn't eat Bert. She was disgusted by it, by the way we'd started to call the patties of meat in the freezer Bert burgers. My sister didn't give a shit about trying to make the best of a bad situation. A lifetime ago she was the girl whose dolls I undressed, whose records I scratched, whose lipstick I tried on. Still, she'd forgiven me. She'd looked after me every day after school. She'd made me snacks and let me watch TV with her. She'd taken me by bus to the hospital and covered my ears whenever my parents' fighting got too loud. She'd smelled smoke and called the fire department when the curtains caught on fire.

"I can't fucking believe you," she said to my mother. "That was her pet. It had a *name*."

At the end of his letter my father wrote:

> I suppose that it's confusing at times and sad too. Well it's the same for everybody. The best thing to do is try to be happy, find some good friends and spread a little sunshine. Sunny is your nickname you know.

So many choices, my father said. To stay in California, to go back to Montreal. I went to Montreal for a summer visit and I stayed into the fall. I was happy and then, like a wave breaking over my head, I was not happy anymore. So many choices, I could not choose. I could not stop choosing. And although I followed his advice, to find friends, to try to be happy, the only decision I made that lasted for more than a few months was not to be called Sunny anymore.

31

I had travelled thousands of miles and lived for months without either of my parents but it was only after meeting Zoe that I began to understand what people meant when they said the word *homesick*.

Zoe was tall, blond and lean. I knew right from the first day at my new school that she was the one I wanted for a best friend, despite or maybe because I could see she was just a little bit of a bully. There were only twenty or thirty kids at the alternative school in Redding, where Molly and I started going while we all still lived on the farm. Then Molly moved away and after the farm was sold my mother and I moved to Redding where the school was and where my sister already lived.

My mother helped pay for my school tuition by volunteering to teach language arts at the school. She had us make our own journals, and we read books about

NEW MORNING COMMUNITY SCHOOL
1720 BRANSTETTER CIRCLE
REDDING, CALIF. 96001
[(916) 241-7091.

To Whom It May Concern:

Sonja Larsen is a student at New Morning Community
School and as part of her curriculum is working with
the Western Service Workers Association doing an independent study in community organizing.

Martha Bean, Director
1-18-78

brave American women and folk tales from other countries. It was the closest thing to a normal class we had. At New Morning School they believed in letting the kids do what they wanted. And what I wanted to do, even more than read, was hang out with my new best friend, Zoe.

I loved the way Zoe's hands could draw anything, and the way she could cry without making a sound like a movie star. She pushed me off the rocks at the swimming hole, and later towel-dried my hair. Her touch was sometimes gentle, sometimes rough, but always possessive, familiar. She taught me how to eat all the crusts off a sandwich first, so you saved the very best for last.

I told Zoe what books to read. I introduced her to Pooh Bear and soon he became one of the leaders of a complex society of stuffed animals we rescued from garage sales. On her back porch we created a home for most of them, a boarding house full of bears and rabbits and other animals. No dolls. We never argued about the rules, because we just knew how it was supposed to be. Once you were the voice of a creature, it was yours for always. You were the voice of its spirit. We got angry when people said we were getting too old be playing games like that. We were not old. It was not a game.

We do other things too. We invent all the letters and sounds of a secret alphabet. We learn too late that it takes more than letters to make a language. We only learn to say our names. Mine is Ya-Kwa-Xee-Bdye-Fel. That's my magic name, the spirit I can summon just by calling. We have secret symbols for our secret magic selves. Zoe's is like a sun. Mine is a circle intersecting another circle. I draw it on a rock and try to remember to carry it with me every day.

I believe in my magic self the way I imagine some people believe in Jesus. That quiet voice that told me things would be okay. I'd heard it before I even knew my true name, in imaginings with my stuffed bear, in the stories I told myself before I went to sleep. This self that was part and not part of the world and, like Jesus, a little powerless but also immortal and all-loving.

Zoe and I make her little sister cry when we collect her hair to cast spells. We are trying to teach ourselves witchcraft from a paperback. We collect hair, finger-nails, rocks and feathers. We believe everything has a power if only you know how to use it.

Once, just to prove we could, we stayed naked all day at school. The whole school, all twenty or so of us, skinny-dipped on our field trips to the swimming hole, so it wasn't the nudity itself that was an act of rebellion. It was the *way* we sat in the common room, defiantly reading. "What?" we said, when one of the staff came in to talk to us. "What's the matter with our bodies?"

But then Zoe, who was a year older than me, went into seventh grade and had to go to junior high. Not wanting to be the oldest girl in our tiny school, I decided to leave too.

I went back to Montreal. I even started school there. Did I go for a visit and stay longer, or did I come back to California for a visit and not leave again? My parents let me choose where I wanted to live but I kept changing my mind, taking turns over which one of them I would disappoint. Wherever I went I was always the new kid in school, starting in the middle of the year, always catching up or falling behind. And whenever things started to look shaky, when the lease ran out or the car broke down, I moved again.

THREE

I burst into tears when I learned that my mother had become a communist. Not because the teacher at my new school had told us that the Commie Russians had warheads pointed *at this very minute* on all major American cities, but because the Russians hunted whales. I had only recently arrived back in Redding from Montreal, where I had attended my first Greenpeace protest and seen a movie about whales that made me cry. Afterwards I signed a petition swearing never to wear lipstick made of whale products. For my last birthday I had received a poster of a blue whale, an ocean mammals colouring book, and even a record of whale music. And now here my mother was sympathizing with their killers.

It was a senior member of the National Labor Federation, a young woman from New York, who explained to me that my mother and she were something called *cadre*, committed communists dedicated to building a second American revolution within their lifetime. She said that the work my mother had begun as a volunteer for the organization was just one part of a larger plan; they were not just do-gooders running soup lines, but revolutionaries, committed to changing the world.

Since we'd left the commune and moved into town my mother had become more interested in feminism, volunteering for the rape relief society and other women's organizations in Redding. At a welfare rights protest in Sacramento she met organizers from the California Homemakers Association, a local chapter of the National Labor Federation.

CHA was organizing women like my mother who, under California's work-for-welfare program, provided home support for the disabled in exchange for their welfare cheques. Even when she worked only the hours she was assigned, she earned less than minimum wage, but often the women she took care of needed extra help. For her and other workfare participants, there were no rules governing safety on the job. Stories of

37

women hurting themselves while lifting their clients out of beds or bathtubs were common.

She liked that CHA brought everyone to the protest, the workers on the picket line pushing their clients in wheelchairs, demanding better benefits for everyone. She was excited by the way they mixed the practical and the political: the soup lines and the labour history classes. In offices in Sacramento, Oakland and LA, they operated food banks, legal and health clinics, free clothing and free welfare advocacy.

Soon the CHA was the only group she wanted to be involved with. She had never heard of a mutual benefits association before, but liked the fact that it was not a charity, or a purely political group, but instead a kind of union for the non-unionized.

And if, later, she was a little surprised to find out that the organization was a recruitment tool for a clandestine party, I guess it didn't put her off. She understood there were tainted words, words no American would have a chance of comprehending if they did not first understand the need for change. The first thing the organization taught in political education classes was about capitalism. How it had to have some people without jobs, how it was designed to always have poor people, to keep some down for the profit of others.

There was something I saw in my mother's face that I would see later in other new recruits. A eureka moment when they understood that being poor wasn't only about bad choices and bad luck. What happened to people, the way they ended up poor and powerless, was not an accident but an essential product of the system itself. But the real discovery was that someday it was going to be different. Since she'd joined, my mother could not stop telling me this. But until I heard the word "communist," I hadn't understood exactly what she meant.

The young woman who used that word about my mother looked startled when I began to cry. She'd been sent to help my mother start an office in Redding. Her name was Pat. Not Patricia or Patti but Pat. In some ways, with her boyish clothes she was very different than my mother, my sister, the Patti from the commune. But in her urgent, serious tone there was something familiar too.

"Slow down, kiddo," Pat said when I started crying. She held my hands. "Nobody's killing whales here."

She told me, "After the revolution, maybe we could ask the Russians to stop, if that's what the organization decides. You could be a part of that."

After the revolution everything was going to be different. The whales, my mother, our daily life. It was all going to be something else. Sometimes I had to remind myself of that in the crowded, smoky office of the newly opened Redding branch of the National Labor

Federation, or NATLFED, as we called it. That this rundown storefront was actually the beginning of something amazing, even if most people who walked through the door didn't know it.

Our branch of the organization was called Western Services Workers Association. The Sacramento and Oakland branches were California Homemakers Association and the Oregon branch was the Northwest Service Workers Association. We were all part of the National Labor Federation and affiliated with a variety of other organizations like the Coalition of Concerned Medical Professionals, and the Coalition of Concerned Legal Professionals. The grassroots activities of each of these organizations—offering medical and dental care, soup lines, food banks, free firewood for families in the winter—were also a way to recruit people to the revolution. After all, who could work on a soup line day after day and believe the system was not broken?

We ran a food and clothing bank in the office and a soup line in the park. Sometimes people came into the office with their faces full of shame and sometimes they settled in like family. And for some people listening to my mom talk about trying to get poor people to come together to fight for their rights was like listening politely to any preacher's sermon at a church soup kitchen. But for other people you could tell it made them see the world in a whole new way.

The office moved several times. For a while we were located downtown near a club everyone said was a gay bar—one night a man walked back and forth along the sidewalk, shouting for the commies and the queers to come out. But the office I remember best was the one located on the edge of downtown. Around the corner was a motel that rented by the month and across the street there was a liquor store.

The only kids around the neighbourhood were the ones in the office and that suited me fine. Even though I wanted this new world my mother and Pat talked about, the daily reality of her work sometimes filled me with embarrassment and dread. Like my sister who had also moved to Redding but lived in her own apartment and took courses at community college, I was anxious people from my school would associate me with the woman knocking on doors or standing outside a grocery store handing out leaflets and raising money.

Even Zoe did not understand, Zoe whose parents smoked dope and whose mother had been in several feminist groups with my mother. I saw Zoe every school day now that we both went to the same junior high. I knew it was going to be different between us. Over the past year, on the rare occasions we'd seen each other, she did not want to build forts or talk in our secret language. Instead she spoke her own language of basketball games and math tests. But I must

41

have believed that when she saw me every day the spell would be broken, that we could go back to our world again, because I was disappointed every day it didn't happen.

I was lucky I loved reading since that's what I did at recess. I didn't even try to make other friends. I was sharing a room with my mom and the rest of the house with half a dozen or more full-time volunteers, a household more regimented but just as crowded and at least as difficult to explain as our days on the commune. At the office there were boxes of donated books. I read a box of Ian Fleming novels. James Bond, Harlequin, Erica Jong, John le Carré, science fiction. Good books, bad books, I didn't care so long as it kept me turning the pages while I waited. Waited for the revolution or for Zoe to come back to me. Whichever came first.

All the friends from my mother's old life—the commune and the women's centre and the rape crisis centre—began to be replaced by people from the organization. She was done with hippies and liberals. *You say you want a revolution*. My mother didn't like that song and she didn't like it when people quoted it as their excuse for not being more political. *We all want to change the world*. That was an excuse and a lie. Lots of people didn't want to change the world, they just pretended they did. My mother had no time for pretenders. "Stop trying to recruit me," Zoe's mother had told mine last time they'd seen each other. We had become too much, my mother and I, my mother with her politics and me with my longing for how it used to be back at New Morning School.

When the revolution came, everything would be different. I imagined my mother speaking before a crowd of people. I imagined my social studies teacher, an enemy of the people, up against the wall in a firing line. The triumphant agreement between Russia and the United States to end whaling. And Zoe greeting me as a hero or begging me to save her, realizing just how wrong she'd been.

FOUR

My mother and I were on a Greyhound bus heading south to San Francisco. I was going on my first trip to the West Coast leadership apartment. They called it a safe house but when we got there it was just an ordinary apartment. Pat greeted us and I understood this was where she lived when she wasn't with us. We were briefed about walking near the windows or going out in large groups and never mentioning the location of the safe house to anyone.

Over the weekend I mostly sat in the kitchen reading and drawing while my mother went to meetings and classes. One night I helped Pat make spaghetti for everyone. As we cooked, Pat explained dialectics to me. Pat said that understanding dialectics was central to understanding Marxist theory. I liked the way she spoke with her hands, gesturing in the air. She explained how everything was made of opposites. Night and day, hot and cold, you needed both for either to exist. Things were always changing, moving back and forth.

"Think about the connection between water and steam," she said, gesturing towards the pot of water boiling for pasta. "They are always changing, one to the other. Water to steam and back again. The philosopher Hegel called this 'the unity of opposites.' The necessary struggle at the heart of all change." I thought about the way things could change, how more often than not they didn't change back again. How Zoe could pretend I didn't exist, or how my parents couldn't even talk on the phone without arguing. But I knew that wasn't what Pat meant. She meant things that couldn't exist without each other.

Dialectics said that there was a connection between the quantity and quality of things too. A single grain of rice is still rice, but we need lots of rice for it to truly fulfill its purpose. Enough little things make a bigger thing. Quantitative change leads to qualitative change.

Pat asked me to try and think of other examples that might be like this, that quantity might change the essential nature of a thing.

45

"Sand?" I said "Snow? Rain? The straw that breaks the camel's back?"

"Excellent," Pat said. "You are a very good student."

As a special treat my mother and I went to the leftist bookstore in San Francisco. You couldn't get books  about dogs or magic in a bookstore like that, but I still liked it, and my mother loved it: the smell of the new books and all the titles by and about women and poor people, all the people left out of history. My mother started to read on the bus ride home but reading in cars or buses made me sick so I looked out the window, sometimes at the world and sometimes at my own reflection in the glass.

Sonja, Sonja, don't be blue, Frankenstein was ugly too. In my reflection I could see that I had my father's broad nose and mother's big eyes, that this don't-be-blue face was a collage of my parents' features, further proof of their incompatibility. And some days everything else seemed patched together too. Some days I was a girl in a safe house learning philosophy. The revolutionary me that only thought about the future. And then there was the school me who just worked on making it through the day. I had three pairs of Dittos, the saddle-backed coloured jeans all the popular girls wore. I'd pulled mine from the donated clothing closet at the office and I lived in fear that someone might recognize them as ones they'd given away. The pants were yellow and blue and brown and so every day I wore some variation of these colours. I particularly disliked the blue and yellow. But when all three pairs were in the laundry I felt like an actor walking on stage without her costume on. As soon as I got home I changed. I didn't like other cadre, not even my mother, to see me in those clothes, just like I didn't want the kids from school to see me in my cut-off shorts and purple canvas tennis shoes standing on a street corner, handing out flyers. Those were two different people, even to me. When we handed out flyers in parking lots, I was careful to look away when kids my age walked by. Sometimes I wanted to be them: popular, normal, stupid. And sometimes I hated them for not seeing what was so obvious: that we lived in a world where some people succeeded only because others suffered. That could change. It had to.

As the Greyhound bus rolled north I thought about what Pat said. Outside the bus, a burned house, an old car, a dog waiting by the side of the road, all passed by. Each thing was in a state of change, a dialectical struggle. Each one had a story. A before and after.

At the office I heard a lot of before-and-after stories. The man who'd been given a lobotomy when he was

47

eighteen. The ex-con trying to go straight. The married couple with minds like children who came by every day. I tried to help the wife learn to read, and in exchange, they let me go to their rooming house and watch cartoons with them. A pregnant teenager who joined the revolution long enough to name her newborn Che, but who disappeared in the middle of the night, leaving her baby behind. Old people. People who were right on the edge of being all right until they lost their job or their kid got sick.

Something terrible had happened to nearly everyone who came through our doors. Some of them didn't even come inside. A homeless man named Shelton camped out on our porch for a month before being coaxed in for a cup of coffee. Another man named Cupcake lived in the abandoned car next to our office, right across from the liquor store. Shelton didn't talk at all but Cupcake had good stories. He'd been a Hollywood extra, mostly in Westerns where his mixed race meant he always played an Indian. Then a horse fell on his legs and left him in a wheelchair.

Cupcake seemed to find us interesting too. "I know what you people are, and I'll tell you right off: when I'm rich, I'm a capitalist, and when I'm poor, I'm a communist. Lucky for you folks I been mostly poor."

After I met Cupcake I watched for him whenever I saw an old Western on TV. For the first time it occurred to me that even the crowd in the background of an old movie was made up of real people. The world was full of stories and telling them was probably the closest I could get to being magic. That was still true, even if my mother was a communist and my best friend looked right through me.

I turned away from the bus window and asked my mother if she thought I could be a writer when I grew up.

"Absolutely," she said. She leaned close so no one else on the bus could hear.

"After the revolution we'll need writers to tell what really happened."

Of all the crazy people that came into the office, my aunt Suzie was the worst. It wasn't just that she was crazy but that she was bossy too. My mother's little sister had been sick her whole life, grand mal seizures as a child, schizophrenic as an adult. My grandmother blamed Suzie's sickness on a brain injury when she was born, badly used forceps that left little dents in the side of the baby Suzie's head. They were gone now, but they'd left their mark.

Even when Suzie was on her medication she was a little scary, with her side-effect tics from shock treatments and years of taking antipsychotics, her tongue rolling in her mouth, the way she jiggled her false teeth

41

or waved her king-sized cigarettes around in gestures of anger or excitement. In an afternoon with Suzie a kid could be accidentally spit on, burned or embarrassed half to death by the things she said and the loud voice she said it in. "Don't ever have a baby," she said to me one day in the grocery store. "It's like shitting out a watermelon."

Her baby, my cousin Dana, was a year younger than me. The first time I remember spending with her was when I was nine and I visited my mother's family in Seattle from Live Oak Farm. Suzie took me and Dana to the Space Needle restaurant for Dana's eighth birthday.

Dana and I were scared in the Space Needle elevator and amazed at how small the world looked from so high up. But what we were most fascinated by was the bathroom. The soft pearly soap that squirted into our hands, and the big mirrors that reflected our images back at us. Hair that had been combed into girlish submission, hers a glossy straight black, mine, brown, baby fine and wavy. Matching velveteen dresses, hers green, mine pink. Our one point of difference was favourite colour: hers green, mine red. But Suzie had refused to buy me a red dress.

We could not stop staring at ourselves. We were magnificent, but we were also in trouble. We were hiding out from Suzie who wanted *more*: more squeals of appreciation, more ladylike behaviour, more love, than either of us had to give. Instead we were giggly, we were bratty, and Aunt Suzie was right: we were *ruining everything*. But we couldn't stop.

Looking in the mirror was like seeing a picture of how it was supposed to be. Two girls who wore matching clothes and went to the same school, where we would be a force to be reckoned with, the smartest in everything but math.

Instead we lived far apart and only saw each other during her court-ordered summer visits to her mother when Suzie was stable, or on family trips to halfway houses or hospitals when she was not. The two girls and their mirror dreams got further away with every visit. We were never going to star on the set of *Zoom* or go to the same school. As pen pals we were erratic. And the price for our good times together was always going to be the bad times with Suzie. Because Suzie was not going to get better even though she always promised she would. Each time I saw Dana, I could see how that knowledge had sunk in a little deeper.

That spring my aunt had moved from Washington and was living in a bachelor apartment not far from the office and occasionally volunteering. My mother had been looking out for Suzie her whole life. In the commune days my mother had brought Suzie to the farm, hopeful that nudity and sunshine and working in the garden would help. And it actually did. But not for long.

51

I could feel my mother hoping again, hoping that the revolution would be a better kind of medicine. I was not hopeful. Suzie tried but the more she tried, the more she wanted back in return. I knew I was supposed to remember that my aunt Suzie was sick, remember the dents that had been left on the side of her head, that she couldn't help her behaviour. But I had been around other sick people. There was a man who visited the commune and talked to ghosts, there were the simple couple and some of the others who came into the office. Even Cupcake, when he was drunk, was nicer than my aunt.

That spring Suzie's bachelor apartment had a pool, and she promised Dana that when she came from Seattle to visit in the summer she could go swimming every day. But by the time Dana arrived Suzie's promise of a swimming pool had turned into another lie. Suzie had given up volunteering and the apartment for a new boyfriend and a two-room residential motel suite on the edge of the town. Instead of a pool, Dana got the bedroom while Suzie and the boyfriend slept on the pullout couch in the living room with the TV and the air conditioning.

We stayed at my house most days, which was better, even though a dozen people lived there, and I shared a room with my mom. We spent our time walking around town, visiting the office, sometimes getting a ride to a park or a pool. We went to a nature sanctuary where she let a tarantula crawl on her arm but I was too scared and for a day or two afterwards I was mad at her for showing off.

Towards the end of summer Suzie started insisting Dana stay with her. At the motel Dana and I slept in the bedroom with the door closed, choosing the suffocating heat over the sounds of Suzie and her boyfriend. We woke up in the mornings already damp from sweat, eyes still sticky with sleep, already tired. Tired of being hot, tired of everything. Everything Dana said was wrong with our town—the weather, the crummy mall, no buses—was all true but it
still made me mad to hear her say it. When fall came she would get to go back to Seattle where she could spend every day after school in the aisles of books at the Different Drummer, my grandparents' used bookstore. And what would I have? A school with no friends. A mother who stood on street corners handing out leaflets. But at least she wasn't Suzie.

Over the course of the summer, Suzie got crazier and crazier. One morning she came running through the motel bedroom door and at first, I thought she was screaming because of her boyfriend. He's going to

53

kill her, I thought. I'm going to witness a murder. But when I opened my eyes it wasn't blood I saw but Suzie's naked and pale white body bouncing up and down on the bed. Not screaming but laughing. Her boyfriend stood in the doorway, sheet half-wrapped around him, face slack with amazement.

Naked Suzie jumping, jumping as high as she could on the motel bed. The radiant white of her skin and the dark triangle where her skinny legs met. Suzie, her body taut with its crazy joy, and the heavy creaking of the springs as she bounced. That was the Polaroid picture, instant, unchangeable, burned into my mind.

"Make her stop!" Dana shouted. I didn't know if she was yelling at me or the boyfriend. "Make her stop."

The night my mother burst into my room to ask me if I thought she should get a divorce, my sister drove her out, and slept with me in my bed. She didn't wait until I asked for help because she knew instinctively what I did not: that if you were older it was your job to protect.

Make her stop. I yelled at Suzie to get out. Maybe she heard me or maybe she just wanted to play some more, but she ran out of the room and we closed and locked the door. But nothing that followed after, coaxing Dana back onto the bed, pulling the sheet up over her, stroking her thick black hair—those simple things that took all my strength—could undo the betrayal of that minute of stunned silence.

———

At the end of summer Dana went home and I went back to Sequoia Junior High. Zoe had moved on to high school and I didn't have to watch for her anymore. But by now the thought of going to school at all seemed pointless to me. After a few months in Grade 8 I dropped out, deciding to become cadre to the organization although technically I was being home-schooled. I read a lot and occasionally I wrote reports on subjects that interested me. For science I learned about the language of whales and the adaptability of urban coyotes, and for social studies I read about the evolution of children's rights. During weekly labour history classes at the organization's office I learned about the Triangle Shirtwaist Factory fire of 1911 that killed 146 workers, the struggle to establish the eight-hour workday and the terrible conditions that farm workers continued to endure in the US. Math was when I added up donations or made change at a bake sale.

But most of my days were spent in the office, making signs, organizing the free-food cupboard, sorting donations of clothing and books, babysitting the children of volunteers and cadre. There were three other kids, younger than me, whose moms were in the organization at the Redding office, and a few who lived in the Medford and San Francisco offices, but I was the only one who'd chosen to be cadre. Being cadre was more than just volunteering time—it was dedication, putting the organization first in all things.

Including my mother and Pat there were eight or nine cadre in the Redding office. Even my mother's boyfriend, Karl, had been recruited.

Karl could fix all kinds of things, including the organization's cars. But Karl, like so many of the others who came through the door, was a little broken. Broken in ways even the others could see. One day he lined up his entire penny collection into a winding, looping trail through the whole house. Some people said he was a genius, so maybe this is just what geniuses did. They had episodes. The revolution had men who could barely write and those like Karl who tried to explain to me just how big a googolplex was. The revolution didn't judge.

Even though I was cadre I knew there was an inner circle that I had not been told about because once a week my mother and most of the other full-timers went to a meeting or a class that I was not allowed to attend and that they wouldn't talk about. I imagined them out in the dark of the countryside, firing rifles together.

All the West Coast offices in the Bay Area and Los Angeles and Sacramento and Oregon got together to attend regional political education sessions every month or so. New and potential recruits were brought to these sessions where sometimes one of the West Coast leadership would give a class and sometimes we'd listen to tapes of a man we called "our friend out East."

My thirteenth birthday fell at the end of a visit by the West Coast leadership. A volunteer named Betty made me a cake and one of the leaders even made me a birthday card, a figure standing on top of the world, holding a gun. Something about the image excited me, made me feel like I was closer to knowing where my mother went during her mysterious night meetings.

Margaret Ribar, the head of the West Coast wrote: *With history on our side, the future is ours. Take it easy but take it!*

My mother wrote: *To my comrade in arms, to the future we are building, because we are strong and determined we will win, much love and solidarity in our struggle.*

Twenty-seven signatures on the card.

You are a guiding light of the revolution.

To the youngest class conscious comrade in Redding.

Pat wrote: *Keep your eyes on the prize.*

Karl just signed his name. So did Suzie. On paper she looked sane, the neatness of her script a sharp contrast to the messiness of her thinking.

By then Suzie had moved into a house with her boyfriend, a real house where both their kids could visit.

57

When Dana visited that summer I was given a little time off from the office, but occasionally I just refused to do my assignments because I wanted to spend time with her. Each time I missed a food drive or a shift handing out leaflets and collecting change for the organization, my maturity and commitment were questioned. I considered giving up my cadre status altogether but I knew that the revolution would be there even after Dana was gone. Dana was less interested in the organization than she'd been in Live Oak Farm or some of the feminist causes my mother had been involved in although she agreed that life was hard for poor people and that things ought to be different.

That summer Dana seemed as unhappy as she always was to find herself in Redding but she seemed calmer, or maybe only distracted. When we were not together she spent her time babysitting the boyfriend's kids, a boy and a girl, who she said she felt sorry for. I thought it wasn't fair but she didn't mind it. There was a boy who liked her in the neighbourhood and he came over a lot. He had family problems, too, and I sometimes teased them that they were pretending to be their own family. She told me there was also someone in Seattle who liked her and I was impressed, but I acted like I wasn't. I didn't think anyone had ever had a crush on me. Boys never noticed me, although men sometimes did. But that did not seem like the same thing.

FIVE

When the revolution came, everyone would have to take a side. Were they a communist or a capitalist, with us or against us? Karl had chosen our side.

Comrades, that's what we were now.

Sometimes, for months, it was as though we'd both forget about what he'd done. Then opportunity and memory collided. Whenever I looked at Karl it was like I was trying to remember and forget at the same time. That he is not who he pretends to be. That I am not who I thought I was. I'm not smart or brave. I'm stupid or a coward or a liar. One day another girl at the commune, just passing through for a summer, asked if Karl had ever touched me. No, I said, mad at her for guessing my secret. She was gone by the time I realized what I'd done, that she must have had a reason for asking me that.

But yes. If anyone asks again. Yes.

The first time he touched me was at the commune, in the morning in my mother's bed. Why had I slept there? A scary dream, a lonely feeling? Karl's hands creeping up my thigh woke up a memory of a field trip when I was five or six and going to French school in Montreal. The bus driver put his hand down my pants. Even though I was learning that there was a different word for everything, I didn't have any words for what happened that day and so I never told anyone.

I try to tell my mother about the bus driver because if I can tell her this, maybe I can tell her about Karl.

"Oh, that can't be right, honey," she said to me. "If anything like that happened I know you would have said something."

Would have could have should have didn't. And now it was too late.

The second time was on the couch in the living room at the commune. For some reason it was just us, so it must have been near the end of our commune days, when everyone else had moved away. Tickling he said. Even the real tickling could be scary, the way he could squeeze the tender part just above my knee, and me, helpless to stop from laughing. Even when he didn't hide what he did to me, no one can see it. Even in plain view, me laughing until I cried.

After a while, I squirmed away from him. But Karl still wanted to play. We pretended he was a cow at the rodeo; I tied him up with a rope, and left him there. I went to the tree house at the top of the hill. From my perch, I could see the house, and I waited to see if he would come and try to find me. But he didn't.

On the communes I'd lived on, the adults believed in telling children everything. If you walked in on people fucking, they might even ask if you wanted to watch. What if it was okay to have Karl's hand between my thighs, what if it was like smoking dope or skinny-dipping, something that only the straight world got uptight about?

Remembering was hard but forgetting was danger-ous. So instead I remembered the number. Two times, he'd touched me two times. And the rules I'd learned to keep myself safe.

No roughhousing alone. Avoid being alone.

But I knew that was all behind us because we were comrades now.

Until a group of us, but not my mom, went to visit the Sacramento office for the weekend. The comrade at the Sacramento office thought that Karl was like my dad and put us in the same bed.

Three is hanging on to my underwear and sleeping on the floor.

It's not just my mother who will lose Karl if I tell the truth. It's the revolution too. Maybe. If anyone believes me. Who would they choose? A grown-up with a savings account who can fix cars, who can fix anything almost. Or me?

I don't say anything.

Four is later that summer when he walked right into my room the night I finally convinced Zoe to come and stay overnight again, four he broke every rule, four she was right in the bunk above me. Four I curled up at her feet crying and tell her about the three times before.

I had spent so long trying to get her to talk to me again. Letters and phone calls and finally, now that we did not go to the same school anymore, she had agreed to see me. It was a start. A start and an end. In the morning we rode our bikes to the hardware store and bought a lock for my door. We didn't talk about the night before. I knew the lock, and the easy way she installed it, lining it all up just right, was the best and last thing she would ever do for me.

"What if there's a fire?" my mother shouted, rattling at the bolted door. "This isn't safe!"

SIX

"Don't get too cynical," my mother said when she hugged me goodbye at the airport. A cynic and an intellectual, those were the two worst things you could be, and my father was both. I didn't know exactly what those words meant, but I knew what my mother was referring to: that not-too-serious way he had about him that might hide anything. What did he believe in? What did he want? Was he happy or sad? I could have told you any of these things about my mother.

My mother had a vocabulary for what she feared for me, *bourgeois, intellectual, cynic,* but my father just had a look, a sigh. I could see it in the mirror and in his face that I could not help but be my mother's daughter in my father's house, idealistic and argumentative, striving. After I moved to Montreal I realized I was on the other side, in another country, maybe even in another social class. After years of living in apartments my father had rented a two-storey house with stained glass and hardwood on a tree-lined street.

I had my own room, which my father's girlfriend helped me paint hot pink. It even had a backyard for my dog, Gemini, a young Doberman shepherd mix I'd gotten not long before I left California, and who for a little while seemed like the answer to all my problems: a new best friend, someone to talk to. Instead her care became another thing my mother and I fought over.

My mother had been sad but also relieved to see us go. Welfare was investigating her for fraud. I'd run away from home with the dog once already after a fight. It was better for everyone for us to live with my dad.

On the outside, my dad's life looked more respectable but it was filled with almost as many secrets as my mother's. He had a job teaching English as a second language but most of his income came from being a supplier to small-scale dealers, marijuana mostly, with a little coke on the side. Once, while babysitting for one of his friends, I'd been given an envelope of two thousand dollars to deliver back to my dad. Another time, when I'd been picked up for trespassing at the country club pool behind our house, I'd seen the relief on my father's face when he realized the police were only there to deliver me home.

I was reluctant to admit it in the occasional and emotional long-distance phone calls to my mother, but I loved my new life. Despite my dad's line of work, the small hum of fear that had followed me everywhere in California was gone. Wasps, rattlesnakes, men in pickup trucks, school bullies, truancy officers, Karl's hands—I'd left all those things behind. And the things I should have been afraid of in Montreal—getting lost in such a large city, not being understood, even my dad getting busted—hardly even crossed my mind.

I loved my school too. My new friends. The math teacher who didn't laugh at me for being so far behind and the lady woodworking teacher and the way the school was half-English and half-French, all of it located in downtown Montreal. Best of all was my language arts teacher, with the real English accent who never told me to stick to books for children my own age, but instead gave me suggestions, and wrote things like *perceptive* and *you've done it again!* in elegant handwriting at the bottom of my work.

He gave the class an assignment to retell a fairy tale. The fairy tale I kept thinking about was Little Red Riding Hood. How she was fooled for the briefest of moments into thinking the wolf was someone on her side, someone she knows, someone who could be trusted. How that red hood was almost like a target on her back. And the intimate way she knew the wolf, the smell of his breath, the moment of revelation from beneath his disguise.

The bus driver.

Karl and the one two three four times.

And what I wrote instead of a story was a poem.

They see the smile
But I see the teeth
You're a stranger
But I know you best.

That poem felt like a discovery, the way in dreams you discovered you could fly or speak a language you never knew. I sent it to Karl and then about a week later, to my mother. I told her about the four times.

Karl replied, writing that he only wanted us to be friends. Despite myself I remembered the treasure hunt he made for me on a camping trip one summer, how every clue rhymed and at the end there were candy bars. I wanted to hate him but I didn't know how to be angry, only sad. In his response to me he'd included a growth chart he'd made, gluing together sheets of paper and copying out the height marks he'd made in the doorway of his old house. *How tall are you now?* he wrote.

My mother's letter came next and when I read it I got the feeling I always did when I was moving away. Like the click of a door closing on a place I didn't live anymore. Like feeling anything was pointless. *Karl and I are comrades now, nothing more.* I read it once and put it away with Karl's letters, souvenirs of things I wanted to forget.

And I do forget. I forget the first paragraph that reads *I knew about that time in Sacramento . . .* I'll fold that truth up and keep those words hidden away even from myself until one day when I am much older and my mother will give me a box of our correspondence. Inside I will find a copy of this letter and proof of broken trust not only with my mother but with memory itself—how even within a single page some things could not be erased while others remained. Also in the box is my response in my big blocky print. *You knew why didn't you tell me.* Where is the memory of writing this letter? Where is the question mark? Maybe the answer was another thing I didn't really want to know.

67

Montreal was my home, not only because I loved it but because I no longer had anyplace else to go. One thing my mother's letter had decided for me was that I had no reason to go back to Redding.

No reason except Dana.

I didn't tell anyone why I'd chosen to live with my father but I sometimes wondered if Dana suspected. In one letter she asked me twice if I had any secrets to tell her. Was it an innocent question about crushes? Or did she have her own secret she was waiting to share?

Dana was always the better pen pal, her letters longer and more frequent, and prettier too, with doodles and a flowing practiced handwriting I could not help but envy.

I'm not in seventh heaven, she wrote when Suzie announced she was pregnant and planned on keeping the baby. Next came the letter about Suzie getting beat up by her now husband and after that another. *Mom's a bit better*—but I didn't know if she meant from the beating or from being back on her medication—*and I'm coping quite well*. I didn't know what that meant either.

PS Write as soon as you can, so you can tell me what's going to happen during the summer. PPS I wasn't trying to sound like a whiny brat (during the letter). It just turned out that way!! PPPS Make your next letter brighter than this one was. That shouldn't be too awfully hard.

But it was hard because my next letter was the one that told her I wasn't coming, that this year she'd have to face Redding and her mother without me. I knew Dana needed me to protect her. But knowing didn't make me good at it. Knowing didn't make me brave enough to go that summer, just like her asking for my secrets didn't make me tell.

Instead I spent the summer immersed in the world of my older friends. The baby of the group, I was the one that had to be taught how to flash her fake ID at the bar and put on mascara.

Don't open your mouth or they'll see your braces.
Wear these heels, they make your ass look good.
Don't forget to tip the waitress.

Through circumstance and what seemed like fate, these friends were the children from the Oakland House and Live Oak Farm and other people my parents met during the start of the commune years. None of our parents were really friends anymore, and they never talked about that life they shared except sometimes with a laugh and a shake of the head. The seventies. It seemed both incredible and normal that years later Molly and I would be standing together in a bar, waiting for the pills we bought in the alley to kick in.

Dana wrote once or twice, her letters short and polite. I wrote suggesting she could come to Montreal. She did not sound optimistic.

By the next summer I'd decided to go to Redding, ready to rescue Dana in my new-found big city armour, spike heels and black eyeliner, the look of a girl who could not be anything but a visitor. While I waited for Dana to arrive in Redding I raided the free-clothing donations and thrift store for costume jewellery and retro clothing. My mother and I stayed in a trailer park with a volunteer and, although it was not mentioned, it was clear that the entire office conspired to keep me and Karl from being in the same room together.

But Dana never arrived. She'd gone on a summer road trip with her neighbours and their young child and she'd refused to come back. And even though that was everything I'd wanted for Dana—a way out of her mother's life, a choice she could finally call her own—when my mother told me that Dana missed her flight home, and no one knew exactly where she was, I could not stop myself from crying because I knew I was never going to see her again.

Over the next year she sent letters, angry, denouncing, to her mother and father, her grandparents, but she never wrote to me again. Sometimes in my bedroom in Montreal I composed long letters in my head and sometimes I even wrote them down. But by then even her dad had lost track of her address. When you left a place, it was better not to look back. I knew that. That was the only way to choose, to let it be the only thing you wanted. Now Dana was learning that too.

My mother told me that when the revolution came everyone would have to choose a side. In 1981 Montreal we were also being asked to pick a side. There was "oui" and there was "non." "Yes" to a separate Quebec or "no." Yes was a new beginning, a recognition that it was different here, not like anywhere else. The franco-phone students and even the teachers at École Secondaire Saint-Luc wore their "oui" buttons proudly, sometimes more than one. Part of me wanted to say "yes" too. I had chosen to attend French high school, rediscover the bilingual girl I had been years ago. I was delighted when my accent fooled people even for a minute into thinking I was Québécoise. But what about the other immigrant kids at my school? What about the people whose skin gave them away, even if their accent didn't? In a basement classroom I get to know the kids from Accueil, the welcoming program for non-French speakers. Chilean teenagers fleeing the Pinochet regime, refugees from Vietnam, countries in Africa I had never even heard of. Would this new nation be for them too? My math teacher called the Vietnamese students in our class "Chang One" and "Chang Two" when he spoke to them at all. I didn't

71

wear any button and when the referendum answer was "non," I felt disappointed and relieved at the same time.

In phone calls and letters my mother said it was going to happen soon, and I knew she meant the revolution. She said that we might lose contact for a while. She didn't know how long.

Your sacrifice right now is your mother's company . . .
Someday, I don't know when, I may be underground and
you might not even know where I am, whether I am alive
or dead . . .

Sometimes I could not think of my mother as more than the revolution itself. She was not Mommy or Pat or Jesse but a woman in a history book, someone who was already gone. But sometimes a memory might pop into my head. Going through the drive-thru on the way home from school. Shopping for school supplies, the sound of her banjo from the other side of the bookcase that divided our room. Such ordinary moments. I couldn't understand why they were so stuck in my mind.

But it seemed like the world was probably ending anyway. Nuclear war might take us all before her revolution ever happened. And this thought, which should have made me sad, made me feel like dancing instead. In gay discos and tiny dance clubs I nursed bottles of beer, was called *la petite Américaine* and tried to pretend that all that mattered was keeping time, dancing in my borrowed shoes, following a rhythm that seemed laid out for me like a gift.

SEVEN

I was surprised but pleased to see my father pull up in front of my music teacher's house, driving his big green sedan we joked was like a narc car. I hadn't been playing long, but I envisioned myself exquisite up on a stage, the spotlight on my gold saxophone—but actually learning how to play was proving to be tedious and disappointing and even carrying the instrument around was harder than I imagined it would be.

But the minute I get in the car, I know he's not there to do me a favour. He's not smiling and the radio's not on. At first I think he's found out I've been going to bars again. Then he takes a deep breath and sighs and I know he isn't even mad, and that's worse.

"I have to tell you something. It's about your cousin Dana."

He looks at the steering wheel and I look at the dashboard, the pebbly green surface of the plastic and think if I get out of this car right now I don't have to know. He won't have to tell me. We will both be happier. But I don't move and my father keeps talking.

"Something happened with that family. They were found in a motel room. She died. They all did. It's confusing."

My father sounds almost angry now.

And then I don't hear him anymore, only the sound of my own voice, crying. It's my fault. For abandoning her. For being happy to see my dad's car. If I hadn't gotten in then she didn't have to be dead, she could just be gone. I already knew that Dana was gone. I'd known when Dana didn't show up in Redding that I was probably never going to see her again.

But the difference between gone and dead is enormous, a shock as physical as a bully's punch to the face. Simply knowing her breath occupied some small space in a shared universe, how could that matter so much? But it did. Every morning when I woke up and every night when I went to sleep. It would not stop mattering.

———

The headline read "Seattle Girl Among 5 Who Died in Motel."

The Frontier motel. I imagined the desert of Arizona, and the Frontier Motel itself. The lights blinking along a motel strip on the north side of town. Vacancy. Free Air Conditioning. And the room. The cheap flowered bedspreads, the plastic on the lampshades. Two rooms they said, so a suite of some kind. I imagined Dana's face, her hair spilled out on the polyester pillow as she lay down one last time. Mostly she had that fierce look, that hungry face she'd gotten in the last summer I saw her. But sometimes she looked happy.

Dana was the fifth victim, identified as a "fifteen-year-old Seattle girl among five who died in motel. Also dead are a family of four: man, woman, a three-year-old girl and a one-year-old boy." When she'd left with them, the youngest hadn't even been born yet. They'd named the baby Marc Dana.

Arizona. Did she ever learn to like the heat? Did she think they were going there for a fresh start or did she know all along? Sometimes I thought about what it must have been like to find them. The violence and the stillness in the room. For some reason I thought a lot about the room. I thought about a wood-veneer nightstand with a nearly new Bible in the top drawer. I imagined a Formica counter with a coffee pot and a hot plate. The stuccoed walls, the texture and surface of the objects inside this motel room. The things that no amount of bleach could ever get quite clean. When did she know she was never going to leave? At some point she agreed. That much was stated in the letter.

The wife was the last one to be seen alive, walking near the motel the day before. She must have known that she was going to die, that her children were going to die. Probably they had already written the letter, worked out the details. Still she took a walk. Still she went back.

The letter said all of those "within the age of reason" had agreed to take their own lives. It claimed they were tired of running from the law, although later it turned out there were only a few warrants against the husband, minor offences. Later we learned he had tried this before, with his first wife and pills.

When the police arrived they assumed that the two people on the bed were a husband and wife, and that the body on the floor was Dana. An officer tells a news conference that the "the last one to pull the trigger is the fifteen-year-old." Then they did the autopsy. The woman on the floor was not Dana. Dana did not shoot them all. Someone tells me her arms were too short to hold the rifle. And the new headline read, "Police Now Say Girl, 15, Was Victim, Not Killer."

Memories of Dana came to me like the station of a radio I could not turn off. All the music we had ever

KURT SMITH/P-I PHOTO

Police now say girl, 15, was victim, not killer

By John Snell

Tucson, Ariz., police said yesterday that they mistakenly identified a 15-year-old Seattle girl as the person who killed four other people and herself in a murder-suicide past this week.

Police had said that Dana E. Greenup apparently used a rifle to kill herself, a former Seattle couple and their two infant children after signing a suicide pact.

But Detective Sgt. Ron Penning of the Tucson Police Homicide Detail said yesterday that it was Mary Jo McKinley, 25, who apparently fired the fatal shots.

Killed were Greenup; McKinley; her husband, Bruce, 28, an unemployed musician; and their children, Jennifer, 3, and Marc Dana, 1.

Autopsy identified woman

Penning said that when police arrived at the scene, they found Bruce McKinley and a woman lying on a bed, each shot through the head. Another woman was found on the floor near the bed, holding an eight-shot, semi-automatic .22-caliber rifle. The two children were found shot through the head in another room.

Penning said police assumed that the woman lying on the bed was Mary Jo McKinley, and that Greenup had the gun. However, an autopsy identified McKinley as the woman on the floor with the weapon, he said.

Penning said a note in the room left no doubt that the deaths had been agreed upon. He said there was no indication that Greenup and the McKinleys were involved in a "romantic triangle," or that the girl's relationship with either of the two was a factor in the deaths.

Greenup was traveling with the McKinleys with the consent of her father, Gary D. Greenup of 514 W. Galer St.

listened to together: Cat Stevens, David Bowie, Gary Numan, Patti Smith. Everything we had ever done together and everything we had ever planned to do.

I remembered the summer Dana and Suzie came to visit us at the commune and although fifteen or more people lived on the farm, they were the only two with me when fire broke out along the railroad tracks across the road. For weeks wildfires had been burning throughout the county. I called a neighbour on the party line since I didn't know how to call the fire department. Then we got my guinea pigs in their cages and headed for the nearly dried-up duck pond. Dana cried as she walked barefoot along the hot dirt road but I said we had no time to go back for her shoes. I don't remember what Suzie did as Dana and I stood in the duck pond waiting for the fire trucks. The trucks came and there was a water bomber plane, too, and within minutes the fire was out. As we walked muddy-footed back to the house, I realized that my plan had made no real sense. But if Dana thought so, she never said anything.

I remembered the day she got her period, and I was jealous, because I was older but didn't have mine yet, and yet I tried to be the expert, pushing her to get Tampax when she said she wanted Kotex pads. In all my memories I was both bossy and helpless.

I remembered how we tried to cut open a Mexican jumping bean we'd bought when we found out there was a worm trapped inside. How we wanted to rescue it. How we wanted to see it. I remembered walking the miles between my house, the office and the motel on the edge of town. All the time we'd spent in an air-conditioned knick-knack shop on the motel mile, inspecting the seashells and coin purses and spun-glass birds and key chains with tiny thermometers that broke when the temperature went above 102. And those memories, fragile and meaningless, were all that was left.

I didn't go to the funeral. Maybe no one invited me, since me with my told-you-so rage was the last thing anyone needed. Or maybe I said no. I didn't want to see the white casket Suzie had asked for, the sugarcake of a burial, the whitewash of a life. Maybe we all pretended it was just as well I didn't go, since money was tight, and I had school exams.

At school, where I was in the last month of Grade 10, I learned new words. Murder, or was it suicide? *Un meurtre ou un pacte de suicide? Ma cousine. Un fusil.* I took final exams about subjects that had no relevance to me anymore in a language that sexed every object; it was all meaningless.

And at home, that two-storey house with its leaded-glass windows and garbage bags of weed in the basement, it was only two months away from my father's wedding to his girlfriend of five years and the party had already begun. Life goes on. Enjoy it if you can. That was the message I interpreted in their attempts to console me with food, with music. One morning my dad offered to drive me to school. We took a detour to the McDonald's drive-thru for breakfast, my dad's one fast-food weakness, and on the way there he rolled a joint, one handed, and lit it up. As he passed it to me I wondered if my dad was always stoned or if this was something he was doing for me because I was sad.

71

It touched everything, this sadness that was sometimes a weight and sometimes an emptiness. It ruined everything. My dog circled me in drop-eared submission to my misery while my friends acted surprised that I was so affected. *How well did you know her?* someone asked. Everything was changing, everything was already different, and all I wanted to do was let Bowie's *Diamond Dogs* play over and over again on my record player, in the prettiest room I ever had, in the house I knew I couldn't stay in anymore, holding my breath while I waited for the needle to drop again.

My mother sent me a copy of *Invest Yourself*, a catalogue that the organization published of volunteer opportunities around the country. There were dozens of the organization's offices listed, in Long Island and New Jersey, Massachusetts and Pennsylvania.

Invest yourself. Those words called out to me. I could be like Dana, a wasted life. Or I could choose to be someone else, someone invested, a force in history.

PART TWO

Revolution is the only solution—there ain't nothing
else. You will obey orders. You have two privileges.
One is to obey the order. The other is to fire the son-
of-a-bitch that gives the wrong order. You've got a clear
choice. Out!

Leaders are leaders because they lead. They overcome what stands in front of them—whether they have
to kick it in the balls, or kiss its ass.

GINO PERENTE'S "ANALYSIS"

EIGHT

He was wearing dark aviator glasses, and a Hells Angels biker vest, with a black T-shirt underneath. The T-shirt read: *Yea though I walk through the valley of death I shall fear no evil for I am the meanest motherfucker in the valley.* He was sitting behind a table at the front of the room with a full ashtray and a stack of notes he never looked at in front of him. It was 2:15 in the morning, and our teacher, the one I'd heard called half a dozen different names—but mostly "the Old Man"—was not showing any signs of letting up soon.

Living in this row of Brooklyn brownstones were nearly a hundred people, breathing in each others' cigarette smoke, building the revolution a day at a time. In this room, what would have been a dining room, we ate and worked and held these weekly classes. We sat on folding chairs, on a couch, on the floor. Still more sat against the walls in the hallway. Occasionally someone's head bobbed up and down as they nodded off then jerked awake. Most people had clipboards in front of them, and some took meticulous notes while others only wrote down the occasional word.

This was National Office Central, or NOC, where for twelve to fourteen hours a day this apartment, and two others in the building, were filled with the uneven *tic-tac* of manual typewriters, some of us typing fast, others slowly, our task to communicate to the field offices what to do. How to hold more profitable bake sales, how to recruit doctors, how to run food banks and winter-clothing drives, how to recruit members, both to the National Labor Federation and to the secret branch whose name I had only recently learned: Communist Party USA, Provisional Wing. In the memos we quoted Lenin and we quoted Marx. But mostly we quoted the Old Man.

Outside was Crown Heights, Brooklyn. In 1981 Crown Heights was a mostly Black and Hispanic neighbourhood of Haitian and Caribbean immigrants In the blocks around us were a dozen storefront churches, holy roller and Santeria, and sometimes in the early evening the sound of singing and crying, in Creole and Spanish, carried from the street. Up on the roof of our apartment, chicken bones, burnt and placed into a circle, had been found, and walking down the street my first day I heard the bleat of a goat coming from an apartment.

Voodoo, someone told me.

The Hasidic Jews patrolled the nearby streets in station wagons, and waited for the Messiah to come. On the floor above lived the last Irishman on the block, an old bagman for the IRA. On the subway, the young Muslims in their long white tunics and with their beautiful serious faces, moved from car to car, cans outstretched for money to feed children, build schools, change the world. And every morning the Catholic church across the street played a recording of bells— bells with just a hint of static. Everywhere there was evidence of our common hunger for a better world, a better life. Here in this city, with its broken windows and needles in the stairways, the sound of gunshots in the distance—everywhere there was evidence that this life would not do.

85

On class nights the Old Man sat at the table with the notes he never looked at, an ashtray, a coffee cup and three cassette recorders that made a small steady whine as they turned around and around. On one side of the Old Man sat Mary T, a petite woman with the pale skin of her mother but the Chinese features of her father. On the other side sat Polly, a taller woman with a thin face and a head of wild curly brown hair. They changed the tapes, lit the Old Man's cigarettes, refilled his coffee. The rest of us sat with our clipboards and notebooks in our laps, trying to write it all down, which wasn't always easy. The Old Man's lessons took twists and turns through all kinds of history, including his own. In one class he might cover events of the Russian Revolution and then move into his own days as an organizer with the United Farm Workers union. Throughout each story were lessons about philosophy and human nature.

The Old Man took a haul off his Lucky Strike cigarette and said, "Truth is the collision of an objective and a subjective reality inside your own mind. For a revolutionary, the truth of the revolution is impossible to deny, since it corresponds to the objective reality of the oppression of the working class, and our subjective concept of justice.

"In other words, kids, there ain't no justice, there's just us," he said, and it seemed like he was looking right at me.

With his dark glasses, and black, slicked hair it was hard to tell how old the Old Man really was. I guessed somewhere between forty and sixty, but I didn't really know. He walked with a limp and had kicked-in-looking teeth, from the Days of Rage riots in the sixties, he said.

In the Genesis document, the organization's official history, we learned that in 1958 "some of our people who joined the Communist Party USA in California . . . became part of a dissident element in CPUSA." I assumed that one of those people was the Old Man, just like I assumed he was in the group that later went to Cuba, and Latin America and then came back to the States. The Old Man seemed to be at the heart of all those stories, although he was never named.

In the short time I'd been at National Office Central I'd heard him referred to as the Old Man, Oldie, Field Commander, Vincent Ramos, Vic Elder, Eugenio Perente, or Gino, but never Jeri, the name that I could see tattooed in faded slanting script on his arm.

I didn't know which of those was his real name. But I knew his voice. I'd been listening to it for years.

Leaning against my mother, my head on her knee, falling asleep as we listened to the tapes from back East in apartments and the back room of the office in Redding, listening and dreaming about what the revolution might look like. My imagination focused on transformed communities: vegetable gardens in abandoned parking lots, sturdy houses with clean windows. But I couldn't picture me or my mother, how old we'd be or even if we'd be alive, after the revolution. And as

I drifted from dreaming to daydreaming to waking, the Old Man's words and the sound of my mother's pen and the rustle of paper as she wrote it all down, followed me.

After the revolution, my mother told me, things were going to get better. She meant that the workers would own the factories, that the wealth would be evenly distributed, but she meant something else too. That we'd understand that it wasn't only our fault; that the powerlessness that had dogged us, generation upon working-class generation, wasn't only because of our failures, but the result of having the weight of a whole system upon us. Someday that weight would be gone.

On those tapes, the Old Man talked about revolutions around the world, about labour history, about Freud and the Catholic church. He talked about Darwin and Marx and Lenin and the rising up of the working class. His voice was rough and disembodied, subject to sudden dips and rises in tone. It was only after I arrived in Brooklyn that I realized that part of the strangeness of his voice was because the tapes we'd received were tapes of tapes, sometimes third- and fourth-generation recordings. In the background I'd been able to hear the coughing and chair rattling of the others in the room, and I knew I was listening to another life, secret and underground.

No one mentioned his name then, and there were many people, like my mother, who did not even know it. *A friend back East,* they said. My mother sat, stiff, on the floor, taking notes in her tidy hand, as the scratchy fuzzy voice talked on.

I was in that life now, the rustle of paper and breath on the audio, the creak of a chair in the distance.

The first person to greet me when I arrived at NOC was Pat. "Hey there, kiddo," she said when she first greeted me at the door. In the three years since she'd seen me I'd changed from a lonely tomboy to an angry and lipsticked sixteen-year-old, but in her jeans and button-down shirt, Pat hadn't changed a bit. When I left Montreal I'd thought I would be going to Long Island, where the organization was founded in 1971. I had an image of myself on a picket line, shouting until my voice ran out. Instead I was taken to the brownstone in Brooklyn where I was happy to see a familiar face.

A few days after I arrived, Pat walked me to the corner drugstore to call my mom. Inside the drugstore it smelled like musk and coconut oil, and boxes of beauty products, waxes and straighteners and lighteners and gels, written in English, Spanish and even Creole, lined the shelves. At the back of the store were two phone booths with old-fashioned wooden sliding doors. Inside each booth, dozens of names and telephone numbers were carved into the walls.

I dialled the operator and called my mother at the office, collect.

"Are you there?" my mother asked me.

I wondered if my mother was trying to picture me: where I was, what I was doing, the way I had each week when she and the other cadre went out for secret meetings. I'd since learned they'd been at their weekly cell meeting, which they held in a church basement. The cell meetings were for the Communist Party USA, Provisional Wing, the secret organization that most of the full-time cadre also belonged to. We weren't affiliated at all with CP-USA, a group the Old Man considered to be sellouts. The provisional was like the IRA's provisional wing, the ones that weren't all talk.

The Party's constitution said you had to be eighteen to join, but the Central Committee had made an exception for me because, in a way, I'd already been FOP, or a Friend of the Party, for years.

Since coming to Brooklyn, I'd learned not only about the inner organization but that "when the revolution comes" was not just an expression, but a *day* on the calendar: February 18, 1984. This was the real thing that made us different than other so-called leftists. There was a plan. There was a deadline. I needed that.

"I'm here," I told my mother.

"And are you in?" she asked me.

Are you in? That was a question my father could never ask me, since he didn't even know there was an "in." He didn't know about the Party, about the revolution. He thought the organization his ex-wife was involved in was a cross between Amnesty International and the Salvation Army. And he thought I was staying in Brooklyn only for the summer.

But my mother and I both knew the truth, that I was leaving Montreal for good. The revolution wasn't like a summer camp you visited. You had to pick a side, eventually. I'd always known that.

"I'm in."

On the way back to the safe house, Pat bought me a slice of pizza. She taught me how to fold it over and tip it in into my mouth, New York style. "Congratulations, kiddo," she said.

National Office Central was really three apartments. The apartment where the Old Man was teaching was the main one. It was where we checked in and checked out every day, ate our dinner, held classes. It was just an ordinary apartment but it was hard for me to imagine any other configuration for it. The meeting room was previously a dining room, and the sleeping room, where we had a double bed and stacked all of our mattresses, had once been a bedroom. There were two large front rooms that now held the desks of the operations manager and political commissar, tables for working, a desk overlooking the street where the watch person sat. Beside that was

91

the Cave, a small room that might have once been a nursery or a closet, which was the Old Man's room.

The organization owned three four-storey brownstones on Carroll Street, twenty-four units altogether. We rented out most of the units but kept apartments in two separate buildings for ourselves, and we had the entire basement that joined them all together. On the ground floor was the organization's law office, which had a reception desk and office in the front room. This area and the Cave were where the Old Man spent most of his time. The rest of the space was used by the organization's three lawyers and any overflow workers from upstairs. One building over was the doctors' office, where the organization's two doctors ran their practice but that we also used for workspace, meetings and sleeping when needed.

In addition to the Carroll Street apartment, the organization had other places throughout Manhattan and Brooklyn. There was a small walk-up apartment in the Lower East Side, an apartment in Park Slope and the homes of supporters who we stayed with overnight. Like most people in the organization, I moved from place to place, sleeping on spare beds, couches and gym mats on the floor.

When class was over we folded up the dozens of chairs, gathered our coats and bags to head off for the night.

Down in the basement I said hello and goodbye to my dog, Gemini. She'd been with me from Redding to Montreal and now New York. It had not occurred to me she would end up in the basement when I brought her here. I only knew I wasn't going back to Montreal and I couldn't leave her behind. Down in the boiler room she'd begun sharing her food with a litter of feral kittens. Back in Redding she'd sometimes take my stuffed animals and surround herself with them— my mother speculated she'd had puppies that had been taken away too soon. When I thought about her down in the basement alone at night I tried to think about the kittens and how we were each doing our work.

I piled into a station wagon with seven other people and we headed to Manhattan. From the car window, I could see a crowd hanging around outside CBGB, the mecca of punk. It was hard to believe I could be so close and yet so far away from it now. Part of me envied the people standing outside in the cold, how they wore their anger in their hair, their boots, their jewellery, the work they put into expressing themselves, right down to the tips of their black-polished fingernails. And part of me could see they looked ridiculous, like actors instead of warriors. Like people with nothing better to do. At the red light, the winos rubbed our windshield with old rags, and even as I looked away from their broken skin and matted hair, I was filled with love for them, my beaten American brothers.

And the only way to show that love was to fight for the revolution.

The roaches scattered as we entered the fourth floor of the Bowery walk-up that was one of the apartments we used. The nights I slept here I pulled the sheet over my head to keep them from crawling on my skin, and still I could wake up with one crushed on my pillow. As the others got ready for bed, I sat down on the sleeping pad and lit a cigarette. Soon everyone else was asleep, their snores another city sound, like traffic.

I sat watching the shadows lose their sharp edge, the light coming through the window a mixture of street lamps and the blue of pre-dawn, that early aching moment that I remembered so well from my last days in Montreal. I coasted from minute to minute on memory and cigarette smoke. My father's car driving up. The moment when I stepped in and everything changed.

I knew when I got to Brooklyn that I was probably going back to the organization for good, that I wasn't looking for reasons to join so much as reasons not to. And I almost found one the day I met the Old Man for the first time. I'd been in at NOC a few days already. Pat said there was someone who wanted to meet me, and she led me downstairs to his office.

It wasn't the rifle leaning against the wall that made me wonder if I was making a mistake. It was the strong smell of Paco Rabanne in the air and the sight of the Old Man in his white suit and a black tie. He looked like a gangster, not a revolutionary. He was sitting behind a big oak desk. I got a feeling that he was waiting for me, waiting to see the look on my face as I walked in. I had an image of myself turning around and leaving, but I couldn't think of anywhere else to go.

He said, "Sixteen, huh? You know, Polly was only fifteen when she became a revolutionary." Polly was in her late twenties now and the political commissar, responsible for education and recruitment. Mary T, another powerful woman in the organization, had been recruited when she was seventeen. He said that young people had fought in revolutionary struggles throughout the world—Spain, Cuba, China. Russia and Vietnam.

I stayed. I listened to him talk, his voice and everything about him both familiar and strange.

"I know you," I said to him.

The Old Man surprised me when he laughed and said, "Of course you do. You're sixteen, you think you know everything. But I know you, too."

My drug-dealer dad, my commie mommy. Karl. My cousin. The scary thoughts in my head when I got too sad.

All the things he knew. He went through them like a list. I didn't have to tell him anything, not even lies.

NINE

"I think I want to stay a year," I said when I returned home to Montreal after my first visit to NOC. I'd already joined and although my dad didn't know it yet, I'd only come back for his wedding and to pack up my things. We both knew asking was just a formality. If he said no, I'd go live with my mother and end up in Brooklyn anyhow. At the wedding I wore a white linen dress my stepmother sewed for me, and in a pair of borrowed pink three-inch heels, I felt almost elegant. The ceremony and the reception were both at the house, and by midnight I was doing lines of coke in my bedroom with a dealer friend of my dad's. While he cut the lines on my vanity I was looking around the room with its hot-pink walls and speakers collaged with photos of rock stars. None of it even felt like mine anymore.

The dealer put his hand on my ass and said, "I want to fuck your brains out."

I liked the sound of that, even if I was already bored with him and the fussy way he lined up the coke on the glass. I liked the thought of someone fucking my brains out. Because that's what I wanted to be, even if for only a moment, if only for this one time in my life: thoughtless and experienced. He was small, only a little taller than me, and slender, and he had soft dark skin but an ugly face. Maybe it was only ugly because I knew I didn't like him. But I liked how he looked at me and I thought it probably wouldn't hurt much for my first time. Still I laughed and said, "Don't be stupid, we'd get caught."

I stayed in the house alone while the newlyweds went on their two-week honeymoon and the day after they left he called me to say he was on his way over. For a minute, I thought about leaving before he got there, but I didn't want to go back to New York a virgin. I stayed and we got high and then we got naked in my father's bed. But he didn't fuck my brains out. He just fucked me, and I was thinking the whole time.

Thinking about Dana and sex, how they said she wasn't sleeping with that guy, but she was, she must have been.

And thinking about the revolution. How it wasn't just an idea. It was a day not even three years away. I'd be almost nineteen then.

I'd been right about the pain, my first time hardly hurt at all. I could see how it might be pleasurable, this friction between two people. Interesting even. But the closeness of the dealer's face, the startling noises he made, like a man wounded, somehow those things caught me shamefully by surprise. I felt better when I saw his look of confusion and fear after he saw the stain on the sheet and got what that little red rose of blood signified. That flicker of panic. He wanted to talk about it, wanted to know why I'd done it but I told him I had a friend coming over and he was quick to leave. I had a bath and took myself out for lunch. And everything about that lunch, the twinge between my legs, the memory of his fear, the quiet moment at the restaurant alone with a book, felt grown up, like it was both the start and the end of something.

That night I turned on the television and listened to the stereos, playing the one in my room and the one in the living room at the same time so that all the rooms in the house were flooded with music. I began going through my records, listening to each one. I stayed up until I could hear the morning birds, and the trucks and cars and the dull roar of daytime from down the block. And for the next week and a half I stayed up all night and slept in the heat of the sun while the phone kept ringing. The little dealer—sometimes to apologize, sometimes to try and fuck me again. Some of my friends called trying to understand why I was leaving. The story I told people was about life experience and living in New York City. The more they tried to hold me to this life, this life where we were just dancing until something terrible happened, the more I needed to leave. But still I went out dancing alone, because after this I knew there wouldn't be any dancing at all.

No dancing, no rock shows. On a whim I went to a Stranglers concert at Club Montreal. I ran into a friend of a friend, and it was as though he could see the change in me. I couldn't stop thinking when I was in bed with him either, but at least I didn't find the proximity of his face so alarming. I slept over at his apartment for two nights. The second night I said I'm moving to New York and he said I know. And the next morning I woke up to Marianne Faithfull singing, *Why'd you let her suck your cock*, and his angry girlfriend sitting in the living room, turning up the volume.

The last person I had sex with was one of my best friends from school. She reminded me of Marlene

99

Dietrich. The high cheekbones and the wave of her hair. Her deep voice with just a trace of a German accent. Sometimes in my fantasies I dressed her up in men's suits or tight skirts. Drunk on the contents of my father's liquor cabinet and the knowledge that I was never coming back, I told her this. We were sad and trembling and clumsy. It was so different with girls. I'd told her all about the dealer and the boy from the bar. She kept whispering in my ear, *Did he hurt you?* I didn't know who she meant but I loved the tenderness, the concern in her voice as she said it.

But even in that moment, against her skin that smelled like baby powder, her body against me like a shield, I was far, far away from all of it. I was watching myself at a distance since I knew none of that mattered anymore.

"What will you miss?" the Old Man asked me when I came back from Montreal with my dog and my trunk of belongings.

What would I miss? *Gone is gone as gone can be, this is so plain but it's hard to see.* That was one of the first poems I'd ever written, when I was nine or ten years old. The things I was aware of missing most tended to be right in front of me. I missed my mother the year she found the revolution, and my best friend when she stopped talking to me in the seventh grade. Still I wouldn't miss that hard-to-breathe kind of feeling I'd woken up with for months, the kind of sad you couldn't dance or fuck away, although I'd tried. And my room in Montreal was just a place where a little girl had once lived. But maybe music, the way a song could be anything: an omen a memory a prayer, the way it could make you feel special, like it was written just for you, just for that moment in your life. I couldn't trust music to keep me safe, to keep me away from Metro tracks or drugs or any of the other places that had been calling to me since Dana's death. But I could still miss it.

"Music," I said.

And he told me to turn the radio on.

TEN

Once a week, the morning after class night, a group of us went to pick up donations around the city. By 6:30 a.m., after a shower and another cigarette, I'd be watching the city roll by from the window of a green cube van. We were on the road eight hours on a bad day and ten to twelve on a good one. The air hummed with the millions of tiny dots that lack of sleep brought and the city changed colours, from the blue to the pink of sunrise to the pale yellow of mid-morning. It was like the all-night acid trip I'd done in the months before joining. My father had made me promise not to buy drugs from strangers, but I did anyway. Acid and mushrooms and THC. They made me throw up but I didn't mind. I liked the empty feeling when I had nothing left inside me and the way I could feel so happy and so sad at the same moment.

We drove throughout the boroughs visiting warehouses, stores, delis, bakeries and butchers who had agreed to give donations. The donations were what fed us at NOC although they were made to the Coalition of Concerned Medical Professionals. We told people that their cheese and milk and bruised fruit was going to malnourished migrant kids on Long Island. I wondered about that lie at first, but didn't those kids need revolution more than charity? Besides, there really was help for them at the field office on Long Island, although what they received was usually not much more than beans and pasta.

On the road anything could happen. Cars loaded with food broke down in inopportune places—Hell's Kitchen, Spanish Harlem. In the space of a year I nearly got caught in a police shootout down an alley and another time I witnessed two men punching a man in the parking lot of a butcher store. The beaten man didn't make a sound except a soft wheeze when he was hit, and for years to come the memory of this scene—how he didn't struggle, his small resigned sound of pain—will come to me at unexpected moments.

My partners on this run were John and Lilia, who were both in their early twenties. John had a little gold earring and was the kind of boy I'd had crushes on at the dance bars in Montreal. He'd been recruited by his girlfriend and they'd both worked in a New Jersey field office, where I'd spent a weekend and attended my first cell meeting. All those years when my mother went to cell meetings I'd imagined her shooting guns, or making bombs. Instead I discovered she'd been sitting around a table in a church basement calling everyone comrade and discussing a list of agenda items sent from National Office Central.

Not long after that weekend John got kidnapped from the New Jersey office by a so-called de-programmer that his parents had hired. They were convinced John was brainwashed. But a few months later he came back, this time to National Office Central. This felt like a connection between us, that we'd been away from the revolution, but returned. We discovered another connection in our old bittersweet memories of rock and roll and recreational street drugs.

Lilia said she'd never taken drugs of any kind. The newest cadre in the office, Lilia was Hispanic, with long dark hair and a round face. She told us that before she joined the revolution, she had thought about becoming a nun. She said she believed all human experience was an attempt to create meaning. You could call it the original sin, or a trick of biology, but in our hearts we wanted order and purpose. She said it in such a resigned tone of voice that I almost felt sorry for her, for the way it seemed like she'd never experienced even the small pleasures of being lost.

I told them about growing up "in the field," and I made them laugh when I told them about coming to NOC for the first time, a little punk wearing red lipstick and a wool beret I'd hoped was suitably revolutionary-looking.

"I was recruited almost before I walked in the door," I said.

My next favourite job after picking up donations was typing directives to the offices. I liked the shape and feel of the different typewriters, the Olivetti and Remington. The whole mood of a day could depend on the machine I got, if the keys felt solid or wobbly, moved smoothly or were stiff beneath my fingers. The difference between a day feeling lucky to have found the revolution and a day when it didn't seem fair that I had to give up my life to fix this fucked-up world.

The Old Man said recruiting people was a numbers game. One out of three people you asked to help out would. Out of three people that had contributed once, one would again. The one-out-of-three ratio went all the way up to cadre status. How many people, how many canvasses and phone calls had it taken to

105

bring us all here? If I hadn't been so bad at math, skipping it that year at New Morning, failing or nearly failing it ever since, I could've probably figured out the answer.

I couldn't do the math but I could remember what it was like looking for that one out of three. What it was like to be a volunteer in a field office. I'd been on bucket drives and membership canvasses and food drives, not just in Redding, but in Sacramento, Medford, Oakland. I knew what it was like to go door to door or stand out in a parking lot, handing out flyers and soliciting donations. When people stopped and took a leaflet, or threw in a quarter, they were surprised to find out I wasn't raising money for Girl Guides or the school band. Scanning the people's faces to see who looked the friendliest, the most likely to give, even though I knew we weren't supposed to do it that way.

I never wanted to go back to Redding, not to any field office. Even though I had committed myself to the revolution the thought of small-town parking lots and bake sales, smiling to try and get a dollar donation made me more frightened than the guns in the Old Man's office.

I still had to do telephone soliciting sometimes, for the donations we picked up each week and I still dreaded it. Just a list of names and phone numbers, and no logical place to start but at the top. I almost welcomed the familiar sound of a dial tone halfway through my pitch because it meant I could stop trying. Even though it was my duty, my obligation, to approach as many people as possible, even though it was arrogance to try and decide who got to hear about the work of the organization and who didn't, there were times I skipped a number because it just didn't feel right. I marked "No Answer" on the sheet.

Typing was easier. I spent a lot of time typing. Most of what we typed went to the field offices. Fundraising pitches, recruitment pitches, drafts of new leaflets. Everything we typed was in triplicate, so after failing two typing classes in high school, I was finally learning to be careful, making sure that my fingers were positioned correctly and that all the edges of the carbon paper were straight. This was my favourite moment: when the paper was lined up and in place, before I'd even started to type, before I hit a wrong key.

We worked all day, taking a break only for dinner. During dinner we put away the typewriters and ate at the same tables, watching the *MacNeil/Lehrer Report* on PBS. Afterwards we cleaned up and put the typewriters back and worked until eleven or twelve at night. When we were done, and if there was no class, we'd go to our assigned sleeping spots for the night.

And that was how it went, most of the first year. Days I went out lifting boxes and thanking strangers. Days I stayed in and typed. Nights the Old Man lectured and nights he didn't. Nights I slept on the Lower East Side, nights I slept in Park Slope.

My mother knew enough to never ask me questions about what I did, but my father thought that I worked at the Park Slope design studio, one of the organization's actual businesses, helping to make advertisements and flyers. From the two or three days I'd spent working there, I knew enough to be able to tell him what it was I was supposed to be learning. Paste-up. Layout. Blueline.

But the reality was that mostly I just slept there, three or four days a week, on a mat underneath a drafting table.

Three women lived and worked there full-time and only women stayed at this apartment. One morning as we were getting dressed, I could see everyone else was wearing the same kind of underwear, pink and green nylon, which had been bought in bulk. The sizes were marked in Magic Marker on the back, to make it easier to find a pair that fit. You could tell I was new because I still had most of the panties I'd brought with me, although now they had my initials marked on them.

That morning the hot water ran out after the third person on the shower list, and on the subway back to NOC Nicole was cranky, twirling her fingers around her unwashed hair in disgust. Nicole had been with the Party eight years—seven in the field and one at National Office Central. I had recently noticed how careful Nicole was about the way she looked. That she applied eyeliner each morning, and often styled her hair. Maybe I noticed these things because, after six months at National Office Central, I had only recently stopped doing them myself. My brief teenage infatuation with girly-ness was over and I no longer wore earrings, or mascara or lipstick; I had not cut my hair since I'd arrived. I didn't need gloss or colour to show the world who I was. I was dedicated, I was cadre, and the face I saw in the mirror—young and a little tired looking—reflected that. It felt like Nicole was trying to pretend she had another life, her curls a kind of defiance.

On the subway back to NOC, each of us was carrying the same style of vinyl overnight bag from a bankrupted travel agency, and I could see that some of the commuters around us were trying to understand our connection. Six white women, plainly dressed, no evidence of religion or politics on our second-hand clothes. But our bags, even the way we stood close together, not talking, gave us away. The rule was we didn't discuss anything related to the organization in public places, and since we didn't watch television or movies, or listen to music or read non-political books, all we had to share were memories from lives we didn't want anymore—or this sleepy silence.

Even if we had talked about the organization, our conversation might have sounded like a code. Everything in the organization had a name, a special name.

101

All of these special names were in a manual called *The Essential Organizer.* The FIN committee raised money. The PRO (short for Procurement) department got stuff: food, clothes, anything and everything. BENE or Benefits, distributed it out to people who needed it. Transportation was the TRX department. There was a name for everything in the organization, a way to do things. A way to ask for donations, or rides, a way to sort the clothes in the free-clothing closet.

As we walked, the six of us, from the subway to the brownstone, we were carrying out the very last fifteen minutes of an eight-hour assignment marked HUS, for housing, on all our schedules. At NOC, every hour in the day was mapped out and colour-coded on a large board. We were nearing the end of a dark grey block on the board that stretched from two a.m. to ten a.m. And when we walked through the door there would be new colours on the board, new tasks beside our names, and the sign on the wall would tell us we were one day closer to the revolution.

It was Day 779 until the revolution and it was also my first New Year's Eve in the Party. On Christmas we ate turkey and took half the day off, but on New Year's Eve we drank whiskey and beer and sang until early in the morning. We sang gospel songs *will the circle be unbroken* and folk songs *this land is your land* and labour songs *there once was a union maid who never was afraid.* But my favourite songs were the civil rights songs that combined the best of everything. *Got my hand on the freedom plow Wouldn't take nothing for my journey now Keep your eyes on the prize, hold on.*

Because I was still a probationary member I had a chaperone, a "shadow" to make sure I had a nice time, someone said—but I knew it was so I didn't get too drunk. My shadow was a tall man named Daniel who was a lawyer and seemed as confused as I was as to why we had been teamed together. He was concerned when I asked for a drink but after I told him I'd been going to bars since I was fifteen and he'd checked that it was okay, he brought me a whiskey sour. I joked that this might be the closest thing I'd ever had to a date, but after that we mostly sang and hardly talked. It moved me to tears, the ninety voices in unison, the three or four guitars and a fiddle, all of us stamping our feet as we sang.

On St. Patrick's Day it was much the same but with more Irish songs and a different chaperone. And again it made me cry. All of us celebrating and grieving at the same time, sad for the state of things, but hopeful for the way it would someday be.

ELEVEN

On my seventeenth birthday the Old Man called me down to his office. He was sitting on the couch. He had on a Western shirt and a bandana tied around his neck. He motioned to a small wrapped box on the coffee table.

"What is it?" I asked

"Open it and find out."

It was a Pelikan fountain pen, black with a gold band around the centre, the kind that fills from an ink bottle. "Why?" I asked him.

"Because you're turning fucking seventeen," he said. "Have a drink. What do you drink?"

What did I drink? Beer from a straw. Southern Comfort. Brown cows. Whatever any stranger at any bar I could get into was willing to buy me.

The Old Man got tired of waiting for me to decide. "Grab the bourbon," he said. The bar cart behind me had a dozen different bottles and glasses on it. "And a glass. Not that glass, a shot glass, you little idiot."

"It burns," I said, after the first shot.

"No shit," the Old Man said, and poured me another one.

"What about you?"

"I don't drink" the Old Man said.

It was the third time I'd met the Old Man privately. The first day when I arrived in Brooklyn, and then again when I officially asked to join.

The Old Man got up to put on a Roy Orbison record. It was old but I liked it. I could picture myself on a dance floor, doing a two-step to some of those songs, thrift store pumps on my feet. My mother and father met in a dance hall, so maybe that explained why it was so hard to let go of what I'd only recently discovered: that I could dance to almost anything.

"Seventeen," the Old Man said. "You look like you're about twelve."

I tried not to let that irritate me, since I knew it was true.

"How old are *you*?" I asked him and the Old Man laughed.

113

"Old. Fucking ancient."

I felt bad about being so flippant, after he'd given me the pen. I picked it up again. "Thank you," I said. "It's beautiful."

The Old Man said, "Tell me about Redding. Did you know I once had a plan to blow up the Shasta Dam? That's right around there. Would've flooded the whole fucking valley."

"Maybe you should have."

The Old Man laughed.

"Why did you want to blow it up?" I asked.

"Just to prove we could, maybe." The Old Man told me that was in 1971 when he was in a group called Largo. I would have been six then, two years before I'd moved to California.

"But blowing shit up is the easy part. Building the revolution, that's what's hard. Why do you think it should be blown up?"

I gave the Old Man my list of reasons. How I knew the first day we arrived there it was not the landscape for me. The heat. The KKK stickers, "Be a man, join the Klan," on the lampposts. Bible freaks. Junior high pep rallies.

When I told the Old Man about my thirteenth birthday party he made me get my birthday card. The card was in a steamer trunk, full of everything I'd brought with me when I came to Brooklyn. I had to ask for the key since the trunk was in a locked storeroom in the basement.

When I opened the trunk, I saw my teddy bear. The teddy bear was the only thing I had left from my life before: before my parents were hippies, before we'd joined a commune or moved to California. Before everything, there was him. Growing up, he was at the heart of games of make-believe so intense I could still hear his voice, soft, woolly and reassuring. He was the only one who'd been everywhere I'd been: on the motorcycle and the bus, or later in my bed when my mother's boyfriend crept in. I almost pulled him out, too, just to rescue him from the dark, but there was no room for him in the three-by-three cubby we were each assigned. So I pulled out the manila envelope of cards and letters, put the trunk back and returned the key.

Back in the Old Man's office I showed him the card. The figure with the rifle, standing on the edge of the world. The signatures of everyone inside.

Twenty-six names. Not just my mother or the other cadre who lived in our house, but the West Coast leadership. Pat, who was now at NOC. A tall skinny man named Charlie who made me the birthday card. Margaret, who would one day take over the Party. The West Coast leaders were in Redding that week, to help give classes and recruit new cadre. Although sometimes the new cadre recruited themselves. The revolution, with its birthday cake and free coffee, clothes and donuts, attracted all kinds of people. People like Shelton, whose signature was the biggest, and

115

looked like a child's, although he was over fifty years old. He came around every day for nearly a year before anyone ever heard him speak, and had only recently started learning to write. Shelton, whose toothless face lit up as he sang "Happy Birthday" to me.

And Robin, recently out on probation, who wrote:

Robin the Hood
hopes you'll be good
and help with chores
and all those bores
and do a good job or you will see
All the bad things that happened to me.

I went over each name on the card for the Old Man. Robin's buddy Delbert, who later that summer told me he'd fuck anything from eight to eighty. Ali and her two kids. They were living in a car until they found the organization. Betty, who was in her fifties but raising the baby named Che, left behind by his teenage mother who'd been cadre just long enough to give birth and run. Fresh from jail, run away, or just rundown, people joined and left every month, sometimes with cash from the latest bake sale or canned goods from the cupboard.

"The lumpen proletariat," the Old Man said. "The social scum. A passively rotting mass thrown off by the lowest layers of old society."

"That's a terrible thing to say."

"I didn't say it, Marx did. How many times do I have to tell you people to stop wasting your time on these losers. We're revolutionaries, not fucking missionaries."

My aunt was one of those losers. The bent, the damaged, the scarred. She'd been sick all her life. Grand mal seizures since she was a baby, all day, every day. Gang-raped when she was a teenager. Crazy by the time she was in her late twenties. Now she was the kind of crazy you could see from a distance, the palsied look of someone who's been on Thorazine too long. Her tidy signature *Sue* on my birthday card seemed like a forgery.

On the birthday card were names of people whose faces I could no longer remember, although I had once called them comrades. And then there were others I could never forget. Suzie. Pat. My mother, who calls me her comrade-in-arms. Karl.

"Karl," the Old Man said. "Tell me about that," he said.

Three shots of bourbon and twenty-six names on an old birthday card.

"Hey there, little girl," the Old Man said. "It's your fucking birthday. You're not supposed to be crying."

By the time I recited the poem for the Old Man, it was not so much a poem anymore as a mantra, a way of seeing the world.

They see the smile
But I see the teeth

"Just tell me what you need us to do," the Old Man said. "Just say the word."

I sat in the Old Man's office, drunk on bourbon and the enormity of the gifts he'd given me.

A Pelikan fountain pen with a gold band and a bottle of ink. The chance to tell a story I had only told myself in numbers, never in words.

I wondered if it might be bravado, the way the Old Man talked, that maybe even if I said yes, the Old Man wouldn't do it. Karl had money and skills, he was useful to the revolution. But he had broken a rule. Leaning against the wall behind the window curtains of his office I'd seen a Thompson submachine gun, an M1-A1, and a shotgun. Karl could be summoned to New York, or more likely killed by someone on the West Coast. Would it be long and drawn out, a trial, an execution? Or would they take him someplace and shoot him in the head, like a mad dog?

I'd been waiting. I'd been holding my breath, waiting, for someone to be angry for me, for someone to name me a victim, and what happened to me, a crime. I just didn't know it until that very moment.

"Just say the word," the Old Man said, but even before I had a chance to think, I'd said no. No to that power, that power Karl had rubbed into my skin, to tell the secret, to destroy the happy lie.

That was the first time I ever said no to the Old Man, and although I didn't know it then, the only time.

The light through the Old Man's window blinds changed from inky blue to pale grey and I was still talking. And if the Old Man was bored, he didn't show it, and if he got confused about the details, he didn't betray that either. I'd discovered something about meeting a person who knows everything about you. What was secret becomes stories, stories I could not wait to tell.

When I got to Dana, when I told the Old Man that one of the ways they realized it wasn't Dana who'd pulled the trigger, that she could not have shot anyone, not even herself because her arms were not long enough, he made me get out a rifle from behind the curtain.

"Pick it up."

"I don't want to," I said.

"Yes, you do," he said. And he was right.

He wanted me to aim it at the wall. That was the first time I'd touched a gun in the Old Man's office.

"Is it loaded?"

"Just do it."

"Up against your shoulder a little more," the Old Man said. "At the picture on the wall. The horizon, aim for the horizon." On the other side of the wall sat a woman at a desk who answered the phones and handled some of the Old Man's paperwork. Would this gun fire through a wall?

"Why won't you tell me if it's loaded?" I asked the Old Man.

"Because this is not a lesson in gun safety."

"Now," he said, "Can you reach?"

And I could.

Bourbon. A fountain pen. The chance at justice. The knowledge that I was big enough, strong enough to hold the rifle; that I was not Dana, and never could be. A chance to redeem myself because I could not save her. Could not or would not, it all ended up the same in the end.

TWELVE

I was excited but nervous about my sister's visit. She had been the only one to tell me not to go to Brooklyn. She'd moved to Seattle and was working as a hairdresser. "I don't know what you're thinking going there," she said.

I wrote up a request asking for time off, my first since I had moved to Brooklyn. After a tour of NOC we took the subway to Manhattan for the afternoon.

She'd been to visit my father in Montreal and then me in New York. Everything about our new lives seemed to make her angry. The happy newlyweds. The way I talked about my work like it was the only thing in the world that mattered. "You sound just like *her*," she said to me. She had always been skeptical about my mother's cause. But the real evidence was my shabby clothes and untrimmed hair. Although she had sometimes rolled her eyes at my thrift-store style in the past, my new lack of interest in fashion concerned her more.

But what could she say? It was too late to talk me out of it, to pretend I was too young. I was the same age my mother had been when she'd had my sister. I was older than Dana when she'd signed the suicide note. The age of reason. I was older than my sister had been when she stayed behind in Montreal at fifteen. Choice was what our parents gave us when they had nothing else to give, not protection, not even sympathy. And that freedom was something they couldn't take back, even if they'd tried.

We walked around until we ended up sitting in the biggest movie theatre I'd ever been in, watching a little creature called E.T. following a trail of candy. *"Again?"* my sister said, disgusted as I stood up to call in to NOC. Even though I had the day off I'd agreed to check in every hour or so. I'd been jumpy, thinking I'd better not get too interested in what was happening to a cute big-eyed freak, this plastic Hollywood creation, because I had this phone call to make soon. And still I could hardly tear myself away from watching him pick up candy in his long fingers.

I spoke with Rena, who answered the phones and typed the Old Man's memos. She had a beautiful red star inked on her shoulder. She was the one I would have hit if I'd accidentally fired the gun through the wall. She put me on hold while she checked what I should do. Then she told me to call again in an hour.

I walked back down the movie theatre aisle, looking for my sister's profile. Everyone could tell we were sisters, even though we didn't have the same dad. But I'd never thought of her as my half-sister. When my mother and father married, my father adopted her, and then they had me. In a way, I was the baby they all had. After the first commune the definitions and the names for Mommy and Daddy may have changed, but she had stayed my sister Patti. And not even all the time we'd spent living apart, sometimes not seeing each other for a year or more, had changed that.

But the revolution, Dana's death, the way she called it murder and I called it suicide, those things stood between us now. My sister was unhappy about my life in Brooklyn but we were good at forgiving each other for things we couldn't change, things like blood and distance. Ideology was just one more thing. Still, maybe that's why we'd chosen a matinee, for a chance to be together without talking. I could remember when I was six or seven, sitting in the dark beside her, waiting for my very first movie to start, eager for some new understanding of the world that only my sister

123

with her platform shoes and rock star T-shirts, could give me.

On the screen E.T. was gesturing to the sky, his big eyes, pleading with the children to help him. And I think that's what made me cry. Not little E.T., who is so far from home, but that the children are able to help him, that they can, that they do. He can be saved.

On the way back to the safe house we took the wrong subway. An elderly black woman on the train told us, "You girls don't want to go this way." We got off at the next station, and waited for the return train, the only white people on the platform. And my sister's frustration at me for not knowing the right way, at the world for being scary, was like a force field around us, holding us together into a family, a flashback to the way it used to be before everything fell apart.

THIRTEEN

All quiet.

I made a note in the log every fifteen minutes, and I wrote down the description of each suspicious car that drove by. *Black late model sedan. Brown van.* In this part of Brooklyn they were not hard to spot. Anything new, anyone white. After months at NOC I had finally been approved to sit on watch duty. I worked several shifts a week, always during the day. I wondered if I would have been approved sooner had I been older. In this way NOC was no different than so many of the other places I'd been before. In my mother's office in

California, at my father's parties in Montreal, always being on alert for the subtle ways older people could assert their power. Each time I sat down for my three-hour shift at the front window I felt as though I had passed a test. I was trustworthy.

Outside it was hot and sunny and a car drove by with its window down, the radio playing a song I didn't know. I watched the street, a woman sweeping her stoop, young men in muscle shirts strolling by and clutching beer bottles wrapped in brown paper bags.

Behind me I could hear the rustling of papers and the clacking of the typewriters.

And every fifteen minutes I wrote: *All quiet.*

Aside from the vote of confidence it symbolized, watch duty itself was enjoyable. The view out the window onto the street, the sense I had of almost being alone, my back turned to the rest of the room. And then there was the time itself. On light watch, when the security threat to the building was considered low, we were allowed to read, to make notes. I wrote in my journal, I wrote letters, I stared out the window at nothing in particular, listening to songs replay in my head.

I wrote a letter to my father. I told him I was doing well. Learning new skills, meeting lots of interesting people. Like most things I'd told my father since coming to Brooklyn, none of these things were lies, but they weren't quite the truth either.

All quiet.

After I finished writing to my father, I tried writing a letter to my mother.

Dear Jesse. I'd stopped calling her Mommy years before, when she'd asked me to, and after Live Oak commune, I'd called both my parents by their first names.

Dear Jesse. Dear Comrade. Before Pat told me about being a communist, my mother never discussed the revolution. She didn't have permission. But afterwards, we talked about it all the time. When the revolution comes . . . When we're in charge . . . After the revolution . . .

What would it be like after the revolution? Everything—too many things to name. We could decide what it would be like, but only if we got there. Getting there, that was the most important thing. When we got there, my sister would understand what we had been working for all this time. She would forgive my mother and me and understand that the organization was different than the communes and the other causes.

I'd cried when I found out my mother was a communist, but I didn't mind the idea of a revolution, a change, not even back then. In the small California ranching town that my mother and I ended up in after the last commune fell apart, there was a dirt-road neighbourhood that some people actually called Niggertown. On a school field trip to the local museum I could hardly tear myself away from the photos of Ishi, the very last

127

man in a tribe of Indians all killed in a single generation. Imagine if there were no one left to understand
you in the whole world? Beside it were artifacts left by
the Chinese, brought in to build the railroad and then
driven out, and just next to that, photos of men hanging
from trees, rough justice for cattle thieves. Every piece
in the museum was proof that this town would never be
home for me. It could all burn in a wildfire or be swept
away in the flood of a blown-up dam, I didn't care.

Except my mother still lived there, she still stood
outside supermarkets, handing out flyers and asking
for change. She collected food and worked the soup
line. And after the office was closed, she sat in crowded
smoky rooms with other cadre and took notes from the
Old Man's lectures. Now I knew that on Sunday nights
she went to cell meetings. I knew everything about her
life. It was my life that had become the mystery, it was
what I knew that couldn't be shared: the Old Man's
name, the safe-house address. In the organization we
frequently signed letters and cards with "Love and
Solidarity." I thought about the two of us, me and my
mom, thousands of miles apart as we counted down
the days to the revolution.

Love and solidarity. It felt like there was nothing
else to write. And so I didn't write anything at all.

FOURTEEN

I had been at NOC for almost a year when the Old Man called me down to his office and said, "Kid, I'm going to give you a job. We're going to knock some sense into this organization. We are going to put in some real systems, some fucking procedures so we can all stop running around like chickens with our fucking heads cut off. I am talking the basic tools, the very basic tools a revolutionary needs. I am talking pens, sweetheart. This whole fucking place is out of pens."

He said we would make an example of the office supply room, we would show people what true organization looked like. He sent me down to the office supply room in the basement to begin categorizing and inventorying all the office supplies we had.

In the basements were change rooms with cubbies—one for the men and one for the women—an office, a workshop, a half-dozen refrigerators and freezers, the office supply room with its floor-to-ceiling shelves, as well as the boiler room where Gemini slept.

I spent the whole day in the office supply room. Gemini came and visited, cautiously followed by some kittens.

It took me two days to do it all. I created diagrams and charts. I made requisition forms, a colour-coded binder, a master list, all according to the Old Man's directions. And then I waited for him to call me again, so I could show him my hard work.

But the next time he called for me, a week later, all he wanted to talk about was French Quebec separatists and hitchhiking across the country. I told the Englishman's secret about the dead pilot, like I knew I always would. We talked about Karl again and Dana. We talked for hours but the subject of office supplies never came up.

Later, back down in the office supply room, filling out the requisitions people had given me, I realized that I was as alone as I'd been in months. Was this another gift of the Old Man's? This time in the basement close to my dog and her new-found family. These hours surrounded by the dusty potential of blank pages and empty notebooks, setting the boxes in tidy lines on the shelf, and listening to music that came drifting in from passing car radios and open windows. All I recognized was mariachi and Madonna. Already I could hear that the pop songs had changed, new singers whose names I didn't know. It was proof of distance from my former life that I didn't have to ask myself who was cool or good, worthy of my attention.

Instead I gathered up pens—black, *not* blue—and yellow legal pads for the Old Man. White-Out and coloured markers for the Control staff who made the weekly schedule, a board that mapped out our week in hourly segments. Office Supply time was a new colour on the grid, a bright pink wedge in my week, a room of my own for a few hours.

Songs from a stranger's radio. The sound of my own voice, humming along. The *thump thump* of my dog's tail on the ground when I said her name. Even though to my sister it might look as if I had nothing, I actually had everything. I had a reason to get up in the morning. I had simple tasks that needed doing. And this revolutionary life I had been on the edge of since I was a child now had a place just for me.

131

Polly called me to her desk. She had a message for me: my mother had gone AWOL. She'd left the Party in the middle of the day, possessions thrown into the back of a relative's car. She'd left a note saying she needed to take care of her father, who was dying of cancer. But her new boyfriend, another Party member, was gone too. "I'm sorry," Polly said. "I'm sure your mother will try and contact you. We can talk about that when it happens." After she told me I went back down to the office supply room. Gemini came over, her tail in a submissive wag as though my tears were something she'd done wrong.

As I stacked paper I found myself remembering a day back at Live Oak commune, after I'd moved to California. Sitting at the kitchen table, carefully cutting out paper flower petals. We were making construction paper posters that said "Dust Is Our Enemy." If China could wipe out the housefly, my mother said, then our commune could live in a dust-free house. Next she showed me how to sweep. She said, "Pretend you are painting a canvas." These were my first memories of her since we'd first joined the communes, since I'd left Lennoxville with Dale. How she re-entered my field of vision, although I had no way of telling how far away she'd been, only that she was back, not just one adult among many, but my mother, holding the broom steady in my hand.

And now she had disappeared again.

Polly was right—a week or two after my mother left, I received a letter from her. She wrote that her dying father asked her to come and stay with him, and she'd promised him she would. In her next letter she wrote that even Lenin knew that not everyone was cut out to be cadre.

I turned over all of my mother's letters—pleading, explanatory, tidy—to Polly. As the head of Politburo she was charged with our political education and morale. My first few responses to my mother were rejected—too angry, too emotional—and over the next few months I wrote so many letters, I could not remember which were the few I'd actually tried to send, and which I simply kept to myself. On watch duty, or just before I fell asleep, but especially alone in the storeroom, I composed and re-composed the things I wanted to say to her.

I remembered walking picket lines with her, falling asleep against her during political education classes. The tone of her voice when she described what life would be like after the revolution. *My comrade-in-arms.* After she left Karl, she told me they were only comrades. My mother who had always understood the pleasure of a new pen, or the importance of lines on a page spaced just right. *Dear Mommy. Dear Jesse. Dear Comrade.* I ran my fingers along the edges of the smooth white paper, and wondered how I was ever going to forgive her.

133

FIFTEEN

"Congratulations," Mary T said with a broad smile. Mary T was petite and her face was a complicated mixture of expressions and features. Amused and annoyed; white and Chinese. She had high cheekbones, almond-shaped eyes and pale skin. Her long brown hair hung down to her hips. Unlike most of us she often wore nail polish and sometimes even makeup, but she chipped off the polish in a nervous tic, and she often chewed her lips, biting off her lipstick. I sometimes wondered what she'd been like as a teenager. I still would have been a little afraid of her.

Even when she was smiling at me I had the sense

that I had done something wrong. I understood that this was her job: to guide me, to keep me in line. Mary T was my sponsor, and we'd been having monthly meetings ever since I joined. Sponsors were your guides the first year in the Party. They helped new Party members understand and adjust to their new life. I'd wanted Pat for a sponsor but I wasn't surprised when I got someone else. Personal relationships complicated revolutionary business. Even as a kid in the field office I'd been able to see that.

Until I joined, Mary T had been the youngest person to join the Party at seventeen. I suspected that the small nudge of satisfaction I felt was matched by an equal feeling of irritation on her part although I knew that my evidence—a way of laughing at my questions, a small smirk she gave me when she was angry—was not very convincing since she was like that with everyone except the Old Man.

My other sponsor was Kiersti, a quiet woman probably a little older than Mary T but less senior. She had short brown hair and was one of the few people in the entire office who didn't smoke. She seldom said anything, but nodded in agreement whenever Mary T said I was prone to daydreaming, to occasional childish behaviour. That if I wanted to be taken seriously then I had to act serious too.

But now that my probationary year was over this would be my last sponsor meeting. Despite their doubts, even despite my mother's defection, at seventeen, I had been accepted as the youngest full member of the Communist Party USA, Provisional Wing.

I had seen the diagrams and read the constitution, but the actual structure and shape of the Party was still somewhat vague to me. As a full Party member I could hold office in the local cell and put forward motions for discussion without the sponsorship of another member. But at NOC the lines between the Party and the National Labor Federation remained blurred. One result was that we did not have weekly cell meetings, as they did in the field—the reasoning being that our cell would be disproportionately influential. Instead only the leaders of the Party, the Central Committee, met, and even then not regularly.

I was surprised when I learned that the woman we all called Struggler was actually the Chair of the Party since it seemed obvious that the Old Man was the leader. But it was explained to me that the Old Man's role as Field Commander was not so much to lead the Party but to lead the revolution that would bring the Party to power. He was like a general in charge of a war.

Struggler was a tall, thin woman with pale blue eyes and short curly blond hair who oversaw most of the day-to-day operations in addition to being head of the Central Committee. In both roles she seemed like an odd choice, with a quiet, delicate demeanour and an almost childlike voice, but over time I saw the resiliency and toughness that lay underneath.

Polly was on the Central Committee too, and there were others I assumed must have been, in particular anyone else who had been around in the early years. But it was never discussed and the structure and rules of the Party did not have much of an effect on our daily lives at NOC. In fact, other than the end of sponsor meetings, the only thing that would change for me was that before I could have left the Party at any time, but full members had to ask for permission to leave. It was both a right and a duty of full members to explain to the Central Committee why their grievances were irreconcilable.

That's what the constitution said, but I had never actually heard of anyone doing that. The truth was people just disappeared the way my mother had done. After seven years in the organization, she'd packed up her things and left with her boyfriend while everyone else was at an all-day event. She'd said she was going to take care of her dying father, which no one quite believed. Why take her stuff, her man even, if she was coming back? "Are you in?" she'd asked me, only a year earlier. But just before I was all the way in, she'd gotten out.

After my very last sponsor meeting was done, I met up with another cadre to cook dinner. Maggie was fun to work with. Tall and blond and apparently related to a prominent family, she had a loud laugh and a relaxed

137

but energetic attitude. We started with the Jell-O, since it took time to set. The food we ate at NOC was straight from a school cafeteria. Maggie and I were making meat loaf with green salad, Thousand Island dressing (ketchup, mayonnaise and relish) and bananas and red Jell-O for dessert. Coffee in a forty-cup urn, and an orange drink we called "bug juice" that came from a restaurant drink dispenser.

We needed more ketchup so we got to walk up to the corner store together. We bought the last five bottles in the store, and Maggie bought me a Coke with her own money. "Congratulations," she said on the walk back. She had been in for five years.

Two other people served dinner, so between the time that dinner was served and the time the dishwashing crew came in, there was a lull where Maggie and I sat alone in the kitchen, having our after-dinner coffee and cigarettes. Maggie's cowboy boots were propped up on the chair, and there was almost a conspiracy of laziness hanging in the air. We knew we could have been scraping pots and stacking pans. Instead we were sitting there, waiting for the kitchen door to swing open and spur us back into action.

At the end of my last sponsorship meeting that morning, Mary T asked if I knew what another right of a full member was.

No.

The right to join the military fraction.

Even as a young girl I'd heard this part of the organization hinted at. Cadre who would be willing to do "anything necessary" for the revolution. But who were those people around me? My mother? That wasn't important. Karl? Pat? I didn't need to know. Things in the organization were on a need-to-know basis.

But now at least it had a name. The military fraction. "Fractions" were all the parts you needed for the revolution, the distinct parts of the whole. The mutual benefits societies, like the one my mother had worked in, were part of the labour fraction. The organization that recruited doctors, put on health clinics for moms and their kids and arranged TB testing was the professional fraction. They were out there—pissed-off doctors realizing that this wasn't enough, that the system had to change. The lawyers visiting clients who had been in jail a year without a trial—the same thing. Like the Old Man said, there was no justice. Just us. This had all been explained to me a year ago in the fraction briefing.

But we all understood the capitalists wouldn't just hand over power. It wasn't logical to think that. So there was the military fraction.

"Would you be interested in finding out more?" Mary T asked.

——

Even in the intimacy of the kitchen, I didn't ask Maggie what she knew about the military. I had been told not to discuss it, but even so it didn't seem like the kind of question I knew how to ask another person. *How far would you be willing to go?* Maybe it was not even the kind of question you knew the answer to until the time came. As my mother's defection had shown, sometimes people changed their mind.

At the end of the night, on the drive to outside housing, me and Maggie and six others were all crammed into a green station wagon like college students pulling a prank, but we didn't giggle. We didn't even listen to the radio, since choosing a channel among so many of us was considered to be a potential and unnecessary source of contention.

Instead of the radio, we told stories. There were two kinds of stories. One story was before.

Before I found.

Before I knew.

Before I joined.

Before she joined, Helen was in medical school, but knowing she could never be a part of that system.

Before she joined, Maureen was getting ready to be married.

Before she joined, Maggie was using too many drugs and living an empty life.

I balanced myself on the knees of bony young women. I could hardly remember this moment, this moment before. I felt like I had always known. Even my father—who did not believe in the revolution, who did not even know about the revolution—did not really believe in the future. If we didn't talk about how a knock on the door from the police could change his life forever, we also didn't talk about careers or college. I had an answer for what to say when teachers or strangers asked what I wanted to be when I grew up— marine biologist, writer, actress—but it wasn't a question either of my parents often asked me.

So I was fascinated by everyone's stories. I wanted to know, was it a sacrifice or a letting go? And what was it like, that wide-open world they gave up? I listened to their voices for clues, since that was something else I could not ask. How could I even word that question? What did it feel like not knowing that most of what they taught in school was lies, that the world was a terrible place, that it was your duty to change it?

The other story we told was after.

After, Helen wanted to help run the national health care system.

After the revolution, Maggie wanted to be the commissar of Florida because she didn't think she could stand another fucking New York winter.

After the revolution, we would all be heroes. We would look back on our lives with amazement at the history we had created. When people said things like this I was not sure if they were joking or not. Maybe it didn't

141

matter. These fantasies were probably as close as we came to imagining not just cadre life, but a life after this.

If I took that next step and joined the military fraction, would I still have that hope that I was going to live through it? That someday my life was going to be different than it was right now? But if I said no, then why was I there? Didn't I give my life to the Party the day I walked in the door? That falling apart, falling-down life of a girl who wanted everything Dana didn't have, including the chance to kill herself all over again. But for something meaningful this time. For something real.

I remembered the unexpected smoothness of the metal and wood of the rifle in my arms, when the Old Man told me to pick it up. The feeling that I had when I held it up, that I had finally arrived at the very heart of things.

Yes, I said to Mary T. Yes, I would be interested.

Revolutionaries shed blood, not tears.

I was twelve when I told my mother that. She was crying on her bed in our shared room. I don't remember anymore why she was crying, or where I'd read that, if I really believed it or if I just thought it was something she wanted to hear. But I remembered how she wiped her tears away and said, "Thank you."

In a locked room on the first floor, Lisa showed me how to take apart and put together an M1-A1. We did this using only a dime, which I had to keep under my tongue when not in use. Lisa was in her early twenties, and said to be related to a member of the Weather Underground. She was tough as nails except when it came to the Yankees and stray cats. She was the Old Man and Polly's aide in the military fraction, and for our training session she was dressed in her full khaki military uniform, with pulled-back hair and a beret. Lisa in uniform had a serenity about her that Lisa in jeans and a T-shirt did not. When she was taking apart a gun, her face had an almost blissful look.

My military time was a new colour on the board. I loved this new way of thinking of myself—as a warrior, a fighter. Sitting on the floor with Lisa, I slid the eight clip into the M1-A1. The gun barrel resting on my thigh, the smooth thin dime in my mouth, the calm look of solemn concentration on Lisa's face as we took the gun apart again and again.

Blood not tears.

That day under Lisa's watchful eye, listening to her careful quiet voice, the pieces seemed to come together like a child's puzzle. I knew the black gun was still only an idea, since I'd never even fired it. But it was an idea bigger and more immediate than forgiveness, more real than love and all its various definitions.

143

PART THREE

Human knowledge is not ... a straight line, but a
curve, which endlessly approximates a series of circles, a spiral. Any fragment, segment, section of this
curve can be transformed (transformed one-sidedly)
into an independent, complete, straight line, which
then (if one does not see the wood for the trees) leads
into the quagmire ...

VLADIMIR LENIN

SIXTEEN

I was sitting at the watch window, smelling the damp cool of early morning. Outside, nothing moved. In the silence of the apartment as everyone else slept I could hear the sounds of an all-news radio station coming from the Old Man's office directly below me on the first floor. Overnight watch was something I did now that I joined the MF section. I could look on the schedule and know who the others were just by the hours they spent staring out at the street, listening for sirens. Me. Lisa, John. A dozen others. The countdown wall was in the low 500s. Less than two years to go.

Aside from night watch most of my military time had been spent reading military manuals, studying diagrams of guns. But Lisa said all my time was military time now, that being an MF cadre meant bringing a soldier's attitude to everyday tasks, leading the others by example. Like being the first to stand up when volunteers were needed to bring in the food or the laundry, or not complaining about cooking dinner two days in a row. It was not easy to do sometimes. To believe, as you folded sixty pairs of pants in a laundromat, that this was important revolutionary work. And yet at other times, it was easy to see this doubt as the remains of my capitalist way of thinking, my own ego getting in the way. What could be more revolutionary than feeding and clothing people, than respecting work that was simple, straightforward, essential? There were no shit jobs in the revolution.

One thing that changed was that I saw the Old Man more often. At his request I brought him pens, his yellow legal pads. And then sometimes he called me for odd tasks. He had a theory that this new disease the Haitians and the gays were getting was a CIA experiment gone wrong. He wanted me to translate the local Haitian newspaper. He wanted to know the words to his Edith Piaf record. Neither of those were in the French I spoke, but I tried my best. We listened to the Piaf album over and over again.

"That's bullshit," the Old Man said. "Nobody lives without regret. Even if it's a useless emotion and we know it. But the worst thing is false regret. That's the fucker. Pretending you're sorry when you're not. That's the worst kind of lie you can tell."

He asked me to learn the words to "L'Internationale" in French:

Debout! les damnés de la terre
Debout! les forçats de la faim
La raison tonne en son cratère
C'est l'éruption de la fin
Du passé faisons table rase
Foule esclave, debout! debout!
Le monde va changer de base
Nous ne sommes rien, soyons tout!

There were words I have to look up like *forçats,* which meant prisoners, and other things I guessed at—the past is a cleared table, or slate, maybe. Mobs or crowds enslaved. But some lines were easy to understand and got stuck in my head for days.

149

Stand up stand up damned of the earth
The world is about to change its foundation
We are nothing, let us be all.

When I came out of the office Mary T or Polly asked me careful questions, to make sure there weren't any orders I was supposed to relay. Did I need more hours in the office supply room? Would he be calling me back later or could I be sent to Outside Housing?

There had only been the one training session with the gun, and then some other reading of military manuals, protocols. I sometimes wondered if it was because Lisa could see that I was not a good soldier, that even in daydreams, with only an imaginary weapon in my hand, I was an uneasy fighter. Although I often imagined firing the rifle, I never pictured a target. There was never someone I felt certain had to die. Sometimes Reagan, but I knew that he was just a symbol anyway. And if not him, then who? Someone whose only crime was to be paid, or tricked or seduced by the capitalists into defending their cause? And yet I often imagined being shot myself. I wasn't sure if I could kill someone, but I did feel ready to die. Didn't that make me a good soldier?

As I watched the street and the rooflines of the buildings around us, counting down the minutes, I was satisfied with the unchanged landscape. Despite chain-smoking and drinking coffee all night, I sometimes fell asleep and was instantly plunged into a dream. Me and my best friend in California, skinny-dipping in a creek.

Speaking French on a crowded bus. Drunken taxi rides. I woke from these small dreams terrified by everything that could happen in a moment. Everything you could miss, everything you could remember.

The CB radio beside me came alive with the Old Man's voice.

"Who's up there?" he asked.

"It's me," I said. "Sonja."

Dialectical theory said that things happened little by little, and then all at once. In tiny increments, life was always changing, minute by minute, breath by breath. In a moment the present became the past, night became day, and who I am became who I was. Evolution said we could not stand still, even if we wanted to. No day was identical to the last; no story was repeated exactly the same way twice. That was one of the lessons of dialectics: that history repeated itself not in tight, identical circles, but in spirals. Everything that happened was brand new but familiar all at the same time.

Hours later, half-asleep, I flickered between dreaming and remembering, trying to understand the exact order of things. The moment before, and the one after.

Bringing the Old Man coffee and a fresh pack of smokes.

His hand brushing my hair back. His hand on my thigh.

No. First was coffee, cigarettes, stories. We sat together on his green velvet couch. He wanted to hear about the communes again, hitchhiking. How long had my parents known Dale, how had they travelled? What were they thinking? His keen memory for details and the questions he asked showed me all the things I didn't know, that I would never know. I remembered the road, I remembered it took us ten days. I knew that much.

I knew that I was a loved baby. Who was born into a turbulent time. That it had been the seventies and a lot of things were falling apart, or coming together, depending on who you were, where you stood. That was the story I'd been told, and the story I tried to tell the Old Man.

But it only took a second for the Old Man to take that away from me.

"Bullshit," the Old Man said. "Pure fucking bullshit."

The hot shock of tears on my skin. The Old Man handing me a fresh cigarette, watching me breathe in the truth of his words, words that washed away every lie, every convenient comfort.

"Just a little girl with big eyes trying to act tough," he said, stroking my hair.

The smell of his Paco Rabanne cologne, the slenderness of his hands, the strength of his arms as he pulled me to him. The voice inside my head that whispered danger. And how that voice went suddenly quiet because there wasn't anything to be afraid of anymore when the thing I feared had already happened.

That was the point, the Old Man said afterwards, as he re-buttoned my shirt. I was like Polly had been when he first met her. Two smart girls so anxious about sex we couldn't think straight. He said, "I fucked her on a desk and made her go back to filing while her knees were still shaking."

When he said that, I was afraid he was going to send me out of his office, back out into the bright crowded world me and the other cadre lived in. My knees were not shaking, but my eyes had gotten used to the darkness of his office. So I was relieved when he told me to pour myself a bourbon, and we fell asleep on the couch listening to the country-and-western station on the radio.

"I think it's pretty, what you and the Old Man have," Polly said a week later when she handed me the birth control pills. Did Polly and the Old Man still have sex? I assumed not since she was handing me the pills. It was two in the morning, and there was no one up but the two of us. I hadn't left NOC since that night. "Pretty" was the Old Man's word. *Pretty, pretty girl,* even though we both knew I wasn't. The Old Man had been calling for me at all hours. Two in the morning, seven in the evening. Sometimes when he called for

153

me he wanted to tell me how to file my office supply requisitions, and sometimes we discussed Quebec politics, hippies, mothers and daughters, life in the field offices, rock and roll and wildfires. Once when he called me he just held out his coffee cup and didn't say a word to me. Often we ended up on the couch. He explored me like a map, naming all the places: my sweet ass, my perky tits, my cocksucker lips.

"What is it?" he asked. "What gets you off?" If my body was a map the Old Man was looking for the hidden treasure.

"It's never happened with anyone" I said. "Maybe I can't. Maybe I'm frigid."

"I don't believe that," the Old Man said. "Do you want to call me Daddy? Is that what you want? You can tell me. Tell me," he said.

But I just turned my head into his bony chest, into the sweet musky smell of Paco Rabanne and Tres Flores, and his pale unwashed skin.

"I don't know what I want."

"I'll help you," he said, his fingers stroking my hair. "I'll help you find what you want."

He said it had been a long time since he'd felt the way he did about me, my intensity, my precocious understanding of the world. *Pretty,* he said, *pretty little girl.* No one had ever called me that before. If pretty was a lie, maybe it all was. I could hear the story that I'd been telling him. Karl, the bus driver, the dealer. I could see the kind of girl I was. There was something in me that called out the secrets in men.

"Maybe you're no different," I said to him. "Just another dirty old man."

He said, "There's the door, don't let it hit you in the ass on the way out."

"How can I trust you?"

"Who do you trust, little girl? Give me one name." He laughed at my silence. "How am I any different? How can I be any different if you won't let me?"

I was curious about the pills he took. "What are those?" I asked. "Are they any fun?"

The Old Man looked at me and said, "You think you're some kind of tough, talking like that. Those pills keep me alive."

"What if you're just a dirty old man. A pill popper?"

The Old Man sighed. "When I'm dead you're going to be sorry you said these things to me."

"Maybe," I said. "Maybe I'll regret it. Probably."

The Old Man talked a lot about death. An assassination, he said, by a government agent, or maybe even one of us. He felt some days like his body might just give out under all the strain. He would often stay awake for four days and then sleep for one.

There were days when he barely ate. Lisa and Polly said this was part of my job now, helping to take care of the Old Man. Polly showed me how to cut the crusts off the ham-and-Velveeta sandwiches, how to wipe the edge of the soup bowl clean with a paper towel. The food had to look nice, to coax the Old Man into eating it. Some days, meal supplement shakes were the most any of us could feed him.

I watched as he drifted off to sleep on the couch. The Old Man told me he was afraid he'd stop breathing in his sleep. I watched the pale, exhausted face, the white roots of his hair shining at the base of his scalp. Lines on his face as sharp as folds of paper, watched his thin chest rising and falling and rising again. I sat and I struggled to stay awake, just to watch him breathe.

I'd had a theory about the Old Man, about the kind of man he was, ever since I'd met him. *I know you,* I'd said to him that first day, and I didn't just mean that I'd recognized his voice. But it seemed like the more I got right, the less it mattered. Maybe I didn't want to be right. Maybe I was tired of being right.

On his wall was an oil painting, a little landscape of woods on the edge of a lake. Pale beech and blue sky reflected in water. The colours of early fall just at the tip of the branches. It wasn't very well done. When I looked at it, I could see the intention of the tree, but not the tree itself. How this line of umber should represent a shadow. The smudge of green standing in for moss. But just in the centre of the picture, the middle of the lake, there was a moment of grace. Perhaps a

three-inch square of something lovely, the clouds per-
fectly mirrored in the surface of a pond on a late
September day.

I'd begun spending hours inside that picture, inside
that landscape of contradictions. Days, weeks. Each
time I lay down on this couch. While he had his hands
inside me, trying to figure out the only secret I had left.
When he'd fallen asleep before he'd told me whether
to leave or stay.

SEVENTEEN

I knew the Walkman was a bad idea but I said yes the minute my father suggested it. He was visiting with my stepmother from Montreal. It was just before Christmas and we were in Times Square, going in and out of electronics boutiques. Finally we had seen them all, and bought a small silver one, and a spare set of batteries. Then to a music store where I bought two cassette tapes: Lou Reed and David Bowie.

I ran through the arguments in my head.

It was a gift.

There were earphones so you couldn't say it was disruptive.

We bought the Walkman. We went to see *Evita* on Broadway. My father thought I would like the show because it had Che Guevara in it, and because one summer we both read *The Return of Eva Perón* by V.S. Naipaul. We didn't talk to each other through books anymore. He didn't know the organization disapproved of Che, who'd gone into the revolution export business, instead of staying in Cuba.

After the show we ate at the Carnegie Deli, and actually sat in a booth behind Henny Youngman, a comedian from my father's era who even I had heard of. We ate in hushed silence, trying to overhear his conversation and it paid off when he said his most famous line: "Take my wife, please!"

The Old Man took us all out to dinner at a fancy restaurant along the river. We rode in a 1972 white stretch limousine. Most days we used the limo to transport people to outside housing, all of us crammed inside, sitting on each other's laps, while we rode around the Bowery getting dirty looks, or having the wheels kicked when we were stopped at red lights. But that night, cleaned out and with only a few of us inside, driving through a better part of town, it felt very different. My father and stepmother liked the attention but weren't quite sure what all the fuss was for.

159

Then the Old Man asked my dad about buying bullets in Canada.

The Old Man had always pressed me for details about my father's drug business. How big? How much? The truth was, I had no idea. My father had been robbed by men wearing ski masks in a hotel in the Maritimes once, so it had to be a little dangerous. There had once been garbage bags of weed in our basement. How much was that worth? In the world of pot dealers was he big or small? I had no frame of reference. Mostly it seemed to me like people dropping by for a beer and some business.

My dad didn't ask what the bullets would be needed for, or why the Old Man would think he knew these things. Instead he said he didn't think that made sense, since the States was where the guns were.

"Why do you think they would be cheaper in Canada? I just don't see why you'd think there'd be any benefit in doing it that way." I felt guilty for the look on my father's face, fear disguised as anger, as irritation. Even though I'd answered all the Old Man's questions truthfully, it was clear that he hadn't really understood that my dad was more hippy than thug.

Perhaps the Old Man sensed that he'd gone too far because he changed the subject and went back to complimenting them both on what a fine job they'd done raising me. How smart I was, how helpful. But by then my dad was very drunk and he spent the rest of the dinner talking about the view out the restaurant window. Where did the river go? And the boats, where were they going? Why did they travel at night? Were there submarines? He was sure he saw submarines.

When we got back to the penthouse, I could hear my father throwing up in the bathroom. Was the Old Man right that I had daddy issues? I didn't want to hurt my father but it seemed like I couldn't help it. My mother's face, the fact that I had lost my card-reading magic, those things would always make him a little sad. And that sometimes made me feel like I had nothing to lose. I put on my headphones and turned up the volume on my Walkman until all I could hear was music.

EIGHTEEN

On my second New Year's Eve the construction paper countdown sign we'd put in the entranceway read "414 DAYS"—414 days until the revolution. This year no one shadowed me and I was distracted by the worry and the hope that the Old Man would call for me, that he would take me from the celebrations or that he would celebrate without me. Near midnight I talked to John, who I hadn't seen much of now that I didn't do PRO runs anymore and slept nearly every night at NOC. I missed the adventure of PRO run days. I think we talked about music, too, and at midnight, as everyone started singing "Auld Lang Syne," John kissed me. I had never had a kiss like it, soft but dry, gentle and without expectation. "It's tradition," John said. Was it? No one had kissed me the year before.

A few days later, the Old Man called me down to his office after class and when I got there he told me to get myself a drink. I poured a shot of Old Grand-Dad, 100 proof. The Old Man chose this as my drink months ago, and I gulped down a few, each in one shot, just like he taught me to do. The Old Man put on some Kris Kristofferson. He was horrified to find out I thought Janis Joplin wrote "Me and Bobby McGee."

"That druggie bitch?" he said and told me to turn up the volume.

When the Old Man asked me about John I felt the bourbon rush through my body like a fever. What did the Old Man know? Had someone reported something to him? I told the Old Man the story that John had told me, how his brothers and his father and a de-programmer roughed him up after they snatched him. I said he reminded me of some boys I'd met in Montreal bars who'd left the farm after their dad beat them up for liking boys.

"Does he like boys?" the Old Man asked.

"I don't know," I said. I said I thought it was brave for him to come back. I didn't say anything about the kiss.

It was getting light out when the Old Man sent me back upstairs. John was sitting in the front window at

163

the watch desk with his back to me, watching the street. Maybe the Old Man planned it that way. That John would sit in the room above us and listen to the low murmur of our voices and the same record playing over and over. Maybe he wanted John to see me, drunk, with the Old Man's smell of hair oil and cologne, worn into my skin. All night, on the Old Man's couch, I'd been wondering this.

I stood in the doorway. "John," I whispered. "John."

Maybe I was crying.

Between us lay the sleeping bodies of four other cadre. In the early morning light coming in through the window, all the sleepers had a shadowy look to them, like bodies painted with watercolours. In the next room, Polly and Struggler slept, as they had for years, side by side on the same pullout couch. And yet this was as close to alone as John and I might ever get again.

"You get yours," he said, not turning around. And the way he said it didn't sound like anything more than the statement of a simple fact.

I sat still while the Old Man took out the shoebox of makeup he kept underneath his desk. It was a collection too large and too random to come from one woman—too many brands, lipsticks in too many shades. I sat on the couch, my eyes closed, as he painted my face. Glossy lips, sparkly silver eyeshadow. *Pretty,* he said, and I wondered if he meant the makeup or my upturned face, waiting for his touch.

The Old Man began telling me new versions, his versions, of the stories I'd told him. The one where I stand by the side of the road, but this time I'm batting my eyelashes, willing bait for the perverts. Dale and the Englishman, the one I called the marshmallow major, what really happened with them?

"Nothing," I say.

"How can you be so sure?"

"Because I'd remember."

"How can you be so sure?" he asks again. In my half-grown body with my nearly grown way of seeing the world it was no surprise to him that I confused men. In his version of the story there was a reason why it had happened to me, why it kept happening to me. I almost wanted to be that dangerous girl he was describing. And when I closed my eyes, I almost was.

Keeping him company. Getting his clothes out. Dusting around the Thompson machine gun, and the rifle, and the .45 that sat on the coffee table. That's how I had begun to fill most of each day. I learned how to fill the Montblanc pen just right, how to lay the crackers around the edge of the soup bowl, how to cut the crusts off the ham-and-Velveeta sandwiches, finish it with a toothpick and an olive. I had to make it pretty so the Old Man would eat something. Polly and Lisa taught me to think of him as a machine, a finicky

165

machine we couldn't fix if it broke. A machine we couldn't replace.

The Old Man rarely slept. He didn't bathe often either. I thought of him as a man whose mind was so active he couldn't be bothered with the meat on his bones, this fleshly life. Even sex seemed like a continuation of our conversations, ideas, concepts taken past words. Or sometimes sex was more like an inconvenient physical need, like sleep, like food. Either way I was useful, special, needed. Most people went their whole lives without meeting someone like him and there were so many ways the story could not have brought us together. Yet it did. We had both walked along the edge of the Shasta Dam. We had both ended up in Brooklyn. Somehow we ended up on this couch where nothing and everything was secret.

One day the Old Man sent me down to the basement to look for a red smoking jacket he had in storage. Judging by the clothes, the Old Man's fondness for costumes and disguises went back decades. A lime green silk suit, a white leather coat. I'd been through five boxes, and hadn't found the jacket yet. I wasn't sure how much of a hurry he was in to get it, so I was torn between re-folding everything and getting through it all as fast as I could.

Joe Hassan was standing in the basement doorway, watching me jump up and down, trying to reach the edge of box number six. Hassan was brought in during

a short-lived strategy to recruit college students directly
to the Party instead of through NATLFED. He was
the spoiled son of some millionaire or diplomat from
Africa. The day the Old Man met him, he brought
him back to Brooklyn and spent days with him in his
office, feeding him ham-and-Velveeta sandwiches and
vodka. I felt a little embarrassed for the Old Man, all
the shouting, and calling for ice until all hours of the
morning, it just seemed like showing off. For all the
intense talk, what was it really? Just to show some rich
runaway that his revolution was worth joining.

"He won't last," I told the Old Man later.

"You don't like him, do you?"

"Not much."

"He's got soul," he said.

I laughed. It was still safe to do that. Laughing,
crying, it was still safe.

I said, "He's got an accent, and a rich daddy." I was
disappointed, perhaps, that we weren't going to ransom
him. Hassan probably would have even gone along with
it. Beyond just eating ham, I was under the impression
he was looking for some thrills, some revenge perhaps.

Instead the Old Man renamed him Joe and put him
to work, mostly on maintenance and carpentry duty.
Every so often the Old Man called him into the office,
and he came out a few hours later, a little drunk and
with new orders: more wood, a better saw. It was like
a game to Joe Hassan, this sweeping and hammering.

167

I was not sure if Joe Hassan was even a Party member, since sometimes he refused to do things. He wouldn't wash dishes, for example, or cook food. Simply would not, and not like new people, who asked nicely not to do something and still ended up doing it in the end. *Women's work,* he said. He wouldn't do women's work.

I'd seen him often down in the basement, his long, thin body in coveralls, his hands white with plaster or sawdust, making shelves, re-organizing the tools. He played the radio, too, a not-quite forbidden thing. He'd let his hair grow long. Maybe he was drying out from drugs. We'd had people like that. He smoked filterless Camel cigarettes, the nicotine staining the smooth mocha ovals of his fingernails yellow. Like the rest of him, his hands were slender and delicate.

As he watched me now, jumping for the boxes, his beautiful dark face was wearing the same smile I'd seen the first day I met him, slightly contemptuous.

"Can you help me with these?" I asked him.

"I see you look at me, you know."

"Sometimes I wonder what you're doing here."

"Maybe I like it." There was sawdust in his hair, and he had the beginnings of a beard. It was hard to tell if he'd gotten skinnier underneath the coveralls he wore.

"The Old Man says you have soul."

Joe Hassan stepped into the doorway.

"Do you want to know what he says about you?"

He put his fingers on my mouth.

"Don't."

"Don't what? Don't tell you? Or don't touch you?"

"You'll get in trouble."

Joe Hassan laughed, almost a giggle.

"No, I won't," he said. "It's his idea."

I pushed past Joe and headed upstairs. Everything that remained of my old life was down in the basement. A locked-away trunk filled with my old journals and my teddy bear, a three-by-three cubbyhole for all my clothes. The quiet, dry order of the office supply room with its envelopes and blank paper. My dog who slept curled up with the cats in the boiler room. And now Joe Hassan, with his lie that might not be a lie, stood in the middle of all of it with that smile on his face.

I knocked on the Old Man's door. The Old Man lay on the couch with his eyes closed. I told him I couldn't find the jacket. The Old Man opened his eyes and looked at me and I hoped he could see from my face what Joe had told me. My little Orphan Annie look, he'd called it once. I wanted to ask him why he'd done it, if there ever was a red jacket, if running into Joe was a coincidence or a set-up. But he just sighed and closed his eyes again, and I started to see that the time for asking questions was over.

169

———

There was a way to do everything. That was one of the Old Man's lessons. It was like the army: there was a right way, a wrong way and an organization way.

There was a way to stack the crackers around the bowl of soup.

There was a way to serve the tea.

There was a way to make an egg.

"Polly," he yelled from the couch. "Look at this girl. This girl does not know shit. Why is that, Polly?" His mouth curled up into a tight sneer. He was pointing at me but he was looking at her. She kept looking from him to me. The look on her face changed as she moved her head. From a hard anger at me, to something soft and questioning when she turned to him. Hard to soft. Soft to hard.

How did I not know shit? I did not even know what it was I didn't know. But Polly's hard look was almost as painful as all of the Old Man's words. I liked Polly, I wanted Polly to like me. She was tough, but not mean, she yelled at people but she never laughed at them. She was smart even though she was a high school dropout and sexy but not very pretty. I liked her because she was exactly the kind of woman I could aspire to be.

We had gone out to Long Island together once, to a dentist who donated his time for one of the organization's field offices. Polly had been fifteen when she became involved with the Eastern Farm Workers Association, organizing farm labourers who worked the

Long Island potato farms. Men, mostly, some of them picked up from skid row and bused out to Long Island to sort potatoes. Overcharged for shelter and transportation, sometimes they made virtually nothing. That was the first field office, and Polly had been with the organization, and the Old Man, ever since. Eleven years.

We didn't talk much on that drive. Polly looked out the window and occasionally pointed out landmarks. Where the organization's first office was, where they put up their first picket. She didn't point out the places she'd lived, or gone to school, or comment at all on the changed landscape, and for some reason that made me like her even more.

I worked with Polly and Lisa almost every day. Helping them get the Old Man's meals ready or wash his clothes. Sometimes three of us together could not get what he wanted done in time. A reference from *Black's Law Dictionary* or a cream shirt with French cuffs he'd worn last year.

The Old Man had never yelled at me, and he wasn't yelling at me now. He was yelling at Polly.

"I guess what I'm wondering, Polly, is how the fuck you think you can lead a revolution when you can't even teach this one small thing."

"I want some education happening here, Polly. Some real fucking political education," the Old Man shouted.

Eggs, sunny side up. That's what he wanted. That was the thing I was incapable of doing.

Seven eggs it took me. Polly standing over me, my hands shaking. Broken yolks would not do. Cut the crusts off the toast and real butter only. Every time. Try it again. Do it again. This egg is no good. You thought it was but it's not. It's too runny. This one is too hard. Throw it away. Try again. The butter is burnt. Three eggs. You've broken it again. Four eggs.

"All I am asking you for, little girl," he said quietly through his clenched teeth, "is to make me an egg. A fried egg. An egg, not runny or crisped at the edges. Do you understand that?" He waited until I nodded my head. "Just an egg," he said gently.

I stood in front of him with the seventh cooked egg. I didn't know if it was perfect or not. The yolk was whole. The edges were not burnt. But was it too runny? Was the texture right? I couldn't tell without touching it. But if I touched it, it might not be perfect anymore.

He wouldn't look at it.

"Pitch it, baby," he said, his face to me not angry now, but drawn, old. "You've missed the point."

A perfect thing. Was it too much to ask, and if it was, why didn't anyone else say so? No one in the office would look me in the eye as I walked through, again and again with the plate. But how could you hope to change the world if you couldn't get this one thing, this tiny simple meaningless thing, exactly right?

———

I was relieved when a few days later Lisa called me down to tell me I'd be spending the night outside the Old Man's office. This was where she usually slept, in case he needed anything. She was not feeling well and the Old Man had told her to take a night off. Lisa had made me a list of what the Old Man might like to eat if he got hungry in the middle of the night. She showed me again where the important books were, *Black's Law Dictionary*, Marx, Lenin, the Bible, and reminded me where his pens and extra legal pads were kept.

Just before she left, Lisa said, "Sometimes it gets noisy. Do you understand? Sometimes the discussions get intense, and it gets . . . Everything you see and hear in these offices is confidential. You're not to talk about what goes on here with anyone. That's only for us."

Only for us.

And only for me to watch Polly as she was called into his office. From outside, the Old Man's angry voice was almost like an animal's snarl, all tone and no words. At first I didn't hear Polly at all.

Only for me to watch as she came out of his office and reached for the riding crop we kept for him on the bookshelf. For months I had been watching Polly as she ironed his shirts or poured his coffee. I watched as she showed me how to rub his boots and his riding gear with mink oil. I had been watching the way that work in her hands looked like privilege. The starch in the cotton, the grease in the whip. When Lisa asked

173

me to fill in for her, I was glad, because I thought after my failure with the eggs that my days of working for the Old Man, working with Polly, were over.

As she walked back into the office with the Old Man's riding crop I kept waiting for her to turn and look at me, for some gesture of acknowledgement. Instead she closed the door and I listened to the soft snap of the whip, and the wincing sound that followed. The small pleading whimpers she made when he began to hit her. There was no way of knowing what was going on inside the Old Man's office, no way of telling what it really meant. Except she let him. Whatever was going on, she was letting him do it.

And I was doing what I was supposed to do. I was waiting, I was listening. I was not saying a word.

NINETEEN

"Shut up," Pat said. "Just shut the fuck up."

The surprise of seeing the Old Man at the morning briefing was swallowed up by the shock of Pat's words, her thin arms and clenched fists and open mouth as she screamed at him. It felt almost surreal, seeing the Old Man in the meeting room in daylight, hearing words I'd never imagined from Pat of all people.

"You never stop. You NEVER shut up," she screamed.

Two men put their arms around her and hauled her out of the room and down the stairs into the apartment below.

After she was gone the Old Man stood up and looked around at all of us.

"Welcome to reality, kids. Not everyone survives this thing. Not everyone one is tough enough to get through it." Then he walked out of the room.

Later that day I was allowed to visit with Pat in the sleeping room. All the lights were off. "I'm sorry," she whispered, but she didn't say what for. I sat on the bed beside her and tried to remind her of that first day—*Remember how surprised I was to see you here?*—and how she took me out for a real New York slice, and showed me how to fold and tip the pizza back into my mouth, New York style. And all those early days in Redding, at the back of the office. How she'd helped me understand dialectics through the steam rising from the stove as we made dinner.

"You said I was a good student. But you were a good teacher."

In the darkness I could hear her moan, curling her body up tighter as she pulled the covers over her head.

And that was the last time I ever saw her. The next morning she was gone. Escaped or let go or something else altogether? I didn't ask. No one talked about the ones who had blue slips of paper marked "Out" by their names on the board that we checked in and out of every day. And when the checkout board was redone in a few months' time, if their names were gone no one asked why.

After she left, the Old Man called me down to his office.

"Pat was difficult for you," the Old Man said. He could see that. Pat was like my mother, someone I could never imagine abandoning the revolution.

He said those things before I could even think them.

We talked all night. We talked about the difference between childish idealism and revolutionary commitment. We talked about what happened to soldiers in basic training, how they were broken down and rebuilt, and that was as close as we came to talking about Polly and the eggs. How not everyone was strong enough to be a soldier to the end.

And in the darkness of his office, I thought about the thousand different ways there were not to be strong enough. You could want things, like music or your own underwear or to hug a dying relative goodbye one last time. You could daydream about things, like taking a bath or spending a day alone or kissing somebody. You could remember people you loved and the life you had. You could forget why you were here, what you were working for. You could try and sleep all day, or not be able to sleep at night. There were a thousand different ways to be weak. But the only way to be strong was to stay.

177

TWENTY

I was sitting on the toilet when Mary T stepped out of the shower. With up to eighty people in the brownstones, it was considered protocol to share the bathroom with the same sex while showering. Her body still dripping wet, her long hair stuck to her back, the first thing she did was dry her hands and light a cigarette.

When I told the Old Man about the Christmas present I got one year at the commune, the lamb I named Bert and how when the commune started running out of money everyone voted to eat him, the Old Man told me Mary T's Chinese father had forced his family to eat the family dog when she was little. He implied this was only one of her father's crimes, that for all the fondling and groping I'd endured, Mary T had suffered much worse. My stories were sad, but hers were sadder.

As she took a long first haul of her cigarette, I saw that her pubic hair had recently been shaved off.

Just like mine.

With the same razor I imagined—the electric razor the Old Man kept in the bottom desk drawer along with the shoebox of makeup. The sight of her honey-coloured skin, tender and uncovered, made me feel like I was falling, like I'd missed a step on a stairway. I had asked about Mary T, but all he would say was that it was different than what he had with me. Different relationship, same razor.

And suddenly I understood the look that she'd given me for so long, half-angry, half-amused, even after I'd stopped being a probationary member and became one of the Old Man's staff. Understanding that she was jealous, I felt a little sorry for her, in a way that I hadn't even after the story about the dog and the father. Only later did I wonder if she felt sorry for me, too, for realizing how things really were.

179

The new girl, Jayne, had the same initials as my mother, JL, and within a month or two she'd taken over my number on the checkout board, a board with slots for each of us. The numbers beside our name were how we called for people over the CB radio between the apartments. Each addition or subtraction of cadre affected which number we had, since we were alphabetically arranged on the checkout board.

Was the Old Man surprised when he called for #25 and she showed up? Not the second time he wasn't. Jayne was another smart girl, Mensa smart and from a good college. But that made it worse. The Old Man worked harder with people from money, harder and faster. I'd begun to see that pattern too. I could smell the Paco Rabanne on her skin as she came looking for file folders and labels. The Old Man had given her the job of re-ordering his files, the same job I'd done only months before.

But then one day her father came and picked her up. Had she called or had he tracked her down? She walked right out the front door. Even leaving was easy for a girl like that.

On my eighteenth birthday, the Old Man gave me a sheer pale yellow blouse that he'd had Mary T go out and buy and I modelled it for him braless, before he fell asleep on his couch.

My other gift that year came from John who gave me a chocolate bar. Happy birthday, Waif, he said, using the nickname he'd given me not long after I'd arrived. I ate it in the bathroom, letting the sweet waxy chocolate melt in my mouth as I cried. One minute I was crying because the revolution was only 329 days away and I might not live to see another birthday. And the next because it seemed like even one more day was too long to wait for things to change.

The batteries in my Walkman began to wear out: the strings on *Street Hassle* slowed and Lou Reed began to sound like he was singing underwater. But it was still beautiful. I'd put in the request for the three-dollar batteries, but instead, after my second request, Politburo asked for the Walkman, since it was so handy for people to listen to classes on. Maybe I knew this would happen, as I tried to hold the button down just right, force Lou to sing for me at a speed close to normal. I knew this like I knew Dana was never coming back, like I knew the day I walked into that office that the Old Man was going to try and fuck me. So maybe the story my father used to tell about me was true, that I was psychic, that I could predict the colour of the card coming up next in the deck.

181

The days on the countdown continued to fall away, and in small, measured acts—burns on her arms and scratches on her face—Barbara was the next to declare herself insane. The night watch reported finding her in the bathroom washing the floor on her knees, saying the Catholic rosary over and over again. She began washing her hands five and six times every hour. First with soap and the next day, with Ajax.

Lisa was assigned to watch over her. Lisa kept her by her desk outside the Old Man's office. Lisa found things for Barbara to do. Fold pillowcases, alphabetize index cards. Polish a boot with a toothbrush. Barbara whispered as she did these jobs, encouraging herself to get each thing just right. The crease of the cloth, the shine of the heel.

But not even Lisa could manage her alone. The first day I saw her there, both Barbara's eyes were black. She had been banging her head against her knees. She was smiling and whistling as Lisa was trying to coax her into giving back a pen she had in her hand. On Barbara's arms were little ink and blood stab marks she had already made. *Hail Mary, full of grace.* She smiled as we bandaged her arms, put peroxide on the match burns she'd made on her legs. We bandaged her head after she hit it against the wall. She smiled, digging her fingernails into her wrists.

The Old Man called me into to his office.

He said something had to be done. He said, "She's our responsibility."

He wanted me to kill Barbara.

It would be the kindest thing, the Old Man said.

Merciful. It happened in war, he said. Not everyone makes it.

"Think about what the alternative is. Hospitals. Pills. Think about that."

I thought about that. My aunt's psych-ward white body jumping up and down on the motel bed. The way she'd made Dana and the rest of us a kind of sad that couldn't be forgotten or forgiven, even though there was no one to blame. After Dana died, she'd jumped out a third storey window. Somehow she survived, but the accident had left her walking with a cane and almost unrecognizable after she'd broken most of the bones in her face. She hadn't been trying to kill herself, she said; Dana's ghost had pushed her. Of all the things she'd said over the years, I believed that one the most. I *wanted* to believe that one the most.

"It's the kindest thing," the Old Man said. "But it's your choice, your decision. This is not an order. It's a request."

Whenever Lisa had to leave her desk, to eat or use the bathroom, she called me to come and sit with Barbara. That was military time, too, guarding Barbara, as she grinned at me through a mask of self-inflicted bruises whispering *Pray for us sinners, now and at the hour of our death.* The blood dripping from a fist clenched tight around an opened paper clip as she began to pray again.

It took me three days to decide.

183

Dialectics was the struggle between opposing forces. Communism and capitalism, sane and crazy, certainty and doubt. You could not fix what would not admit to being broken, you could only overcome it, destroy it. Destroy it and believe that from its ashes would come another kind of life, a better kind of life.

The Old Man said whatever I decided he would understand.

And I said yes.

TWENTY-ONE

Outside the world was white. I sat by the window and watched the snow fall over Crown Heights. The courtyard below was white and clean as though no one had ever walked there before. I felt high from all the Sudafed I was taking. I'd had bronchitis for weeks. Every breath I took I could feel the small protest in my lungs. Nothing was simple anymore, not even breathing. I took another pill.

Across the courtyard I thought I saw a man watching me from behind a pair of red curtains. Some days I thought I could see the flash of a gun. There were less than a hundred days left.

I turned back to look at the room. Mary T was sitting in the corner, reading over the polemic one of the field liaisons has typed up. She rubbed at the side of her face, in a distracted kind of way, running her fingertips over the bruises on her cheekbone. In parts, it was a dark wine purple, and others, a softer burgundy.

What had she done to make the Old Man so angry? I'd only ever seen people with bruises like that when they were caught trying to leave. There had been a few of those, runners caught halfway down the street. But no one in leadership, not even Polly, whose legs and back had been struck with the whip, had ever shown a bruise before—but then she only took showers late at night when everyone else was asleep. I couldn't imagine Mary T either trying to defect or being stupid enough to get caught. But still she had the only thing I would have punished her for, that small half-smirk. Only Mary T could wear a black eye like a mark of status.

The empty courtyard. Mary T's hands on the bruise. The flutter of the curtain. Once you started watching you could never stop.

Who was it that was watching me watch them? The NYPD, the FBI? Who knew about us, about what we did in this house, this house we called safe?

Barbara had been a test of some kind, but had I passed or failed? I remembered looking at the guns in his room, the olive green room, and wondering which one would be used. The one I'd choose for myself was the Old Man's silver .45 pistol, since it was intimate but certain to get the job done. I didn't know how it would happen. I hoped Barbara wouldn't be afraid, that she would know the act was from love.

A day or two after I told the Old Man I'd do it, Barbara was gone. I woke up and there was a blue slip by her name, and that was the end of it. Maybe the Old Man killed her himself. I didn't think so. I didn't think anyone had, although for the first time I let myself imagine fully what it might have been like. If she struggled, if she did not accept her fate, if the gun wobbled or the shot was overheard. Was Barbara dead? And which was I more afraid of believing? That the Old Man was a killer, or that he'd never meant it at all, that he was a liar?

I didn't know.

I didn't want to know.

It was an act of faith or defiance, to turn my back to the window, to look away from the clean snowy emptiness of the concrete yard, and return to the smoky clutter of the room before me, to face the room with its three work tables and seven manual typewriters. The sign at the front door that read "Check Out with Control."

187

That was me.

If Barbara was a test, this was another kind of test. To take the girl who failed math from Grades 4 to 10 before dropping out altogether, and make her Control, put her in charge of logistics. Every night ask her to divide sixty-three cadre into five apartments using six cars. Subtract who is slowly going crazy, who is looking for a way out. Subtract who is new and exotic. Divide potential lovers and other suspect alliances. Factor in the twelve who can drive stick, take away the twenty who have not left this apartment in years.

At the Control desk, I made the lists, I marked off the names. On the schedule board that was bigger than my desk, the hours were marked in coloured squares on quad-ruled paper, a row for each of us. And on the wall beside me was the checkout board with a blue slip by Barbara's name.

When I'd first arrived at NOC, the blue slips on the checkout board had intrigued me most. The slips were colour-coded by location and time stamped with the big industrial stamper that sat by the desk. Yellow for the first floor, green for the basement. Blue for all those who were Out. Nicaragua, I'd thought in the beginning, guerrilla training camps, clandestine meetings, secret trips in the dead of night. But I'd learned that usually blue meant AWOL. Blue was the colour of their childhood bedroom in a New Jersey suburb, or the vein in the arm when they were tying off. Blue was where people went when they stopped being here.

Six slots on the board had new blue slips in them.
Joe Hassan got picked up by men in a black limo one
day, by what we assumed were rich relatives. Love
affairs were revealed when two people disappeared
overnight. We found Gemini tied up outside the supermarket after the woman we'd sent out to buy butter
never came back. That was the end of going out alone
for all of us, even with the dog.

At the beginning of the fall we were eighty in the
safe house and the surrounding area. By winter we were
sixty-three. Two women in the last month had been
caught trying to get out, and were beaten for it. But
mostly people did get away and we threw out everything they left behind. Half a dozen in the few months
since I became Control, including the woman who'd
been Control before me. People said they were going
down to the basement for potatoes, and they ran out the
back door. They jumped out of cars at stoplights, they
stepped out of a subway car at the wrong stop.

"Out" I wrote on a blue tag by their names.

After a week or so I began to black them from the
cadre list and the call lists for the CB radio and the next
time we updated the checkout board, a lot of us had
new numbers again.

Six thousand, one hundred and seventy-four hours
each week. Each hour was mapped out, coloured in.
And yet still we struggled. Still we were running out

189

of time. A lost hour could never be recovered. And on my lists, these new black lines that covered over the names we never said again.

Pat. Barbara. Lisa.

Maybe a month after Barbara disappeared, Lisa followed. She was on an all-night watch; we didn't even realize she was gone until the outside housing crew came in and woke us all up.

When Lisa left, the Old Man got the limo and a couple of his main guys and went out looking for her. It almost made me jealous to think of the Old Man looking through the tinted windows for her face on a street corner, even if I knew probably what he wanted to do was kill her. I wondered if he would ever do that for me.

The last time I went down to the basement, I saw the cats she'd been feeding. They scattered in all direction when I walked past them, swollen-faced with pink eye, hissing and mewing. Some of them had already gone blind. I didn't know what to do. I added this to the list, the list of things I did and didn't see.

The milky blue stares of blind cats.

The shine of metal from a courtyard window, the flicker of a red curtain.

The smudge of his comb-in hair dye on a woman's shirt.

The shifting colours of the bruises along the edge of Mary T's broad cheek.

———

When I made my logistics, I started by writing down those who always stayed behind at NOC. Polly, Struggler, Mary T. Most of the men stayed. I stayed. I pressed down hard on the paper, making four copies of each sheet.

Then I marked off who was going to outside housing: the loyal but unimportant, the emotionally stable.

And lastly I worked through the rest of the names, those who presented a problem of some kind. People getting too flirtatious or too close, someone caught crying in a bathroom, someone new or who had caught the Old Man's attention. Assigning transportation and beds to the question-mark cadre was the longest and most complicated part of my job. When I was done, I passed the lists on to Mary T, the first of three people who approved them every night.

It was a class night so I had to hurry to get the lists cleared before class began. I started in the late afternoon and by the time I finished, the last of the light had faded from the courtyard and it was time to call everyone for dinner. The shifting light through the window, the sound of my voice echoing through all the rooms as I announced dinner over the CB radio: these were the small pleasures of my day. Since I'd been assigned to Control I sat at this desk every day for fifteen hours or more, leaving only for bathroom breaks and to get my clothes from the basement. I ate at this desk and slept on the couch right beside it. Outside, the

201

courtyard was street light and shadow, snow and stone and even when I turned my back to the window, I could hear on the CB the sound of the falling snow, the soft whisperings of static.

It was two in the morning by the time class was over and people crowded around my desk, looking for their list of cars and travelling companions, one leader and one list to a car, all of them eager to get started before the weather got worse.

"There's no one else?" John asked, looking over his list. "There's no one else on here that can drive?"

The dark shadows under his eyes and the way he held his cigarette, tight to keep it from shaking, told me how exhausted he was. It was two a.m. now, and he'd have to be up and on the road by six-thirty tomorrow morning. Even a nap in the car from here to Manhattan would help.

Lately I'd found myself remembering the days when I still did PRO runs. Being outside, witnessing the world. Driving in a cube van along the East River, watching the sun on the water and drinking coffee from waxed paper cups, thinking I was going to make it all different.

I didn't do those things anymore. I didn't ride in cars, or sleep in different places. I didn't wake up every day to a new block of colour in my life, a chance to read maps or have conversations, or sift through reams of paper in the basement. I didn't do dishes or cook.

Not even for the Old Man. I didn't wash the Old Man's clothes or polish his boots. Instead, I ate and slept and worked in this room, in this corner of this room. A window, the couch that I slept on, a desk. My life had become a monochromatic strip called Control.

On the clipboard before me were dozens of names, thousands of combinations. Sometimes I looked back at my old sheets, to see if I could duplicate what I'd done before, if somehow one night could be made to look like any other. But it never quite worked. Every day I had to start over. Factor in who was newly arrived, who was exhausted, who was coming down with the flu. Calculate who had left recently, and the domino effect of this departure. Who was lonely, who'd been left behind? Measure fatigue, stress, depression; from each according to their abilities, to each according to their needs.

Calculate his kiss like a small electric spark. No one had ever given me that kind of kiss, simple and empty of expectation. John, whose lips brushed mine for the briefest of moments, dry warmth pressed against my surprised mouth. A New Year's tradition, he'd said. Not at NOC it wasn't. Or his birthday present. Estimate the risk. The risk of remembering these moments, of wanting more. Once you started, it was hard to stop. Music, chocolate, tenderness, fresh air. More.

Even if I'd tried to schedule someone else to drive, to save John from that job, Mary T would have changed

193

it on the list, as she had half a dozen times before. She had a keen eye for favours, generally, and I suspected kept an eye on me and John in particular.

"You're it." I said to John now. "You're the only driver there is."

I hardly looked at John anymore. I looked at his hands, at the edge of his face. John was right. I got mine, and he couldn't rescue me from it. He would've been crazy to try. But I wondered what he thought it was exactly. What did I get? The status as one of the Old Man's special girls, occasional nips of bourbon, beauty makeovers and storytime. And if it was mine, if it was what I deserved, staring into the perfect square inside the picture on the Old Man's wall, too sleepy to even pretend at pleasure, then why didn't I have it anymore? Why was I now exiled at the Control desk, in the corner of this room, scrambling to get us from point A to point B and back again?

I woke up in the morning to see Beth as she hurried out of the kitchen and down the stairs, a big tray held out before her. Beth did my job now. Since Beth started cooking for the Old Man, he'd gained ten pounds. Beth knew how to make eggs Benedict and lobster bisque.

I sat at my desk in the corner and watched her go. Let her, I thought. Let her count down the days to the revolution by cooking, by stirring hollandaise sauce for her beautifully poached eggs. Let her future be caught up in every moment of that act, let that be her measure as a soldier, as a woman. Never get good at something you don't want to do, my mother taught me. It was a lesson she said she learned from my father. And I didn't want to make the Old Man's eggs, I didn't want to oil his riding crop. I didn't want the complicated gift of his skin on mine anymore. That's what I told myself, and maybe it was even true.

After Jayne left I took back looking after the files, and after Lisa left, I took over some of her work ironing his shirts and handwashing his clothes. I removed the women's underwear I found pushed between the cushions on the Old Man's couch, a worn cream-coloured polyester pair with tattered lace around the crotch. Their used-up sexiness made me sad. But I left the half-full jar of Vaseline underneath the couch, the pink coiled hair of Susan, NOC's only remaining red-head, still embedded inside.

Spoiled Jayne and prissy Susan who brushed her long red hair one hundred strokes a night, and now Betty Crocker Beth. Even the clearest memories I had seemed suspect. What about Rena with the red star tattoo or Lisa, with that look of concentration on her face, the careful way she pronounced each word as she went through the pieces of the gun. Were their khaki uniforms like the lipstick and eyeliner, just another one of the Old Man's dress-up games? Was that why they'd left?

As I measured out the minutes in the day, reminding people when it was time to move from one task to another, summoning cadre and dispatching cars, there were dangerous leftover moments. To sit and watch the wind blow through the trees, and what might be the shadow of a man behind the red curtain across the courtyard. To study my own reflection in the window. Minutes when I realized I was waiting, not just for the revolution but an end to these small treacherous observations. The passage of time. The movement of women in and out of the Old Man's office.

I had taken to laying my wrists against the heat of the radiator, keeping the veins against the heat for as long as I could while I counted and recounted, named and renamed.

The ones I knew: Polly, Mary T. Me. Jayne. Beth. Susan.

The ones I wondered about. Lisa and Struggler. I could not imagine either one, but maybe that didn't mean anything. The ones I suspected: The new girl who'd escaped leaving my dog tied outside a supermarket. Or Linda, a tough-looking girl but painfully shy with long curly hair she kept constantly twirling with her fingers.

Linda usually slept at the Lower East Side apartment, where she worked with John, calling businesses to get donations of food and money. The Old Man called her down after class one day, and started keeping her for days running at NOC. She spent those days sullenly carrying out minor tasks while she waited for the Old Man and she had a look of dread when he finally did call her. What might have been a gift for me, a chance to tell it all, to leave nothing out, was a punishment to a girl like Linda. It surprised me that the Old Man couldn't see that.

I made a point of sitting by her at the next class time. I had seen her before, her pen on paper, taking energetic notes. That night when I looked over at her notebook she was writing out page after page of lyrics to Bruce Springsteen songs.

"Candy's Room," "Badlands" and "The Promised Land."

Had she been doing this all along, all these months, or was this something new?

"What did you say to her?"

That's what Polly and the Old Man wanted to know after Linda left the Lower East Side apartment a few days later with a backpack full of canned goods.

"What did you say?"

I said I didn't remember, and that was the truth. I remembered wanting to sit beside her, and the look of the lyrics, the way she wrote out the whole chorus in neat schoolgirl script. I remember thinking I might have reacted differently that first time, if I'd known that

117

I was one of many, or that being special would prove to be so difficult, and so fleeting. But maybe not. My track record for saying no was not very good. And anyhow maybe Linda didn't need me to tell her that.

Polly walked me down to the telephone on the ground floor and sat looking pissed off while I dialled the number for Linda's family. The Old Man was just assuming I'd said something to her, because I'd sat beside her two days before she left. If they actually knew I'd said something to her, things might be worse. If I said anything at all. Still I had to make the calls.

"Is Linda there?"

"I have an urgent message for Linda."

"Can you tell Linda it's very important she contact me?"

The voice on the other end of the phone said she wasn't there, and I believed him. I thought about Linda and the missing cans of tuna and baked beans. Not the baggage of a woman going home to her loving family.

One message. Two messages.

"Can you tell me where I can find her? There's something I need to tell her."

I didn't even know what it was I was supposed to say. For two weeks I kept calling. Three messages. Four and five.

Had I said anything? I didn't remember saying anything.

Now I sat in the corner at the Control desk and I made the lists, all the lists, and I stroked the soft pink burn marks on my wrist when no one was looking. Reminding myself of my skin, my veins, the choices I still had the power to make.

Polly. Mary T. Me. Jayne. Beth. Susan. Maybe Lisa. Maybe Struggler. The new girl. Linda.

And Tanya.

It wasn't just my imperfect egg or Linda's defection, or Beth's bisque, but Tanya and how one night the thing I knew I must not say flowed out of me as though I'd been rehearsing for weeks. That's what got me into this corner, this public exile, my "promotion" to Control Officer.

"Tanya's too young," I'd said to the Old Man. I do remember saying that.

Tanya was fourteen or fifteen. A true Party kid. Her dad and her mom ran a field office in Oregon, and I'd met her there for the first time when she was ten and I was thirteen. She'd come the previous summer to visit her grandmother and aunt who lived at NOC and stayed ever since.

Tanya lived in limbo between kid and cadre. I did not think she was a Party member since she seemed to pick and choose assignments she liked. Cars mostly. She had a crush on John H, the tall blond mechanic who'd recently become one of the Old Man's right-hand men, after his previous one went AWOL. Already Tanya had spent hours in the Old Man's

199

office, sometimes along with John H, sometimes alone.

"That's too young." I said to the Old Man. "You know that, right? I don't know about you and Polly, but this time you'd be making a mistake. She's a tomboy, a kid. I'm not saying that because I'm jealous."

And I wasn't. I'd kept my mouth shut about Jayne, and Susan, and, despite what he believed, Linda.

When I'd said that, the Old Man didn't get mad, but he got tired awfully fast. He had me fix him a bowl of chocolate pudding, and then he went to sleep. After a while, he woke up and asked me what I was still doing there. That was in the fall and not long after, I was re-assigned to the Control desk.

Tanya's grandmother didn't seem worried about the attention the Old Man gave to Tanya. She called him the Old Man, too, even though she was clearly older than he was. I was pretty sure she was a Central Committee member although her job at NOC was to train the cooks and run the kitchen.

Tanya's aunt, Diane, was a different story. I could see it in her face whenever Tanya was called down to the Old Man's office. I could see it in the way she stroked the scar tissue that covered her throat and chest, the way she always did when she was stressed. Years earlier she'd been shot in the chest by a man. They had to do open-heart surgery to keep her alive. But she survived, she told me, because that's what she was. A survivor.

Diane also worked in the Control department. Each

week she mapped out the schedule, colouring in each of the tiny squares, according to the information she'd been given. When the woman who ran the department before me went AWOL, Diane carefully coloured herself in for the job the next week. Senior Control Officer. But instead that job was given to me, younger and with less seniority in the Party.

"I see how this works," Diane said to me when she found I'd been promoted over her. Did she? When Tanya got called down to the Old Man's office, I watched Diane's hands run up and down her neck and chest, a secret code for the not-so-secret way things were. I sat at my desk. Tanya ran down the stairs. This was how it worked. But even if the tips of her fingers against her survivor's skin were saying something neither of us was quite willing to admit, I didn't think I'd let a comment like that go again. It would only take a word from me to Polly or Mary T or maybe even the Old Man himself. Only a word for her to be transferred, or lectured, or maybe even slapped. I hoped she could see that too.

I'd earned this place that might be exile or may be another gift. It was mine, this corner of the room, this window, the voices of strangers drifting in over the CB radio. Truckers and neighbourhood patrols, taxicabs and lonely men. In the Yiddish I couldn't understand, and the southern drawl of a trucker who called himself Green Eyes, I felt as though I'd found a secret hiding

201

place. It wasn't music, but it was something. It felt like any moment the voices would speak to me, tell me what to do.

For months I'd spent nearly every day at my desk in the corner of the room. Days went by and no one said my name. Not even my initials, SL. Control, they called me. I thought some days that the Old Man had forgotten who I was, even though he knew everything there was to know about me. That he'd forgotten where I was, even though he put me there. And every time I heard his voice on the radio I found myself hoping and dreading that the number he would call for was mine.

Control. This is what he gave me. Watching Tanya and Polly and Mary and Beth go up and down to the Old Man's office when he called for them, and teaching myself to be concerned only with the shifting holes in the day created by their absence.

When I first came to NOC I thought: now I know everything. The safe house, the voice on the tapes, the Old Man's many names. Everything, I thought. But I'd come to understand how foolish that was. I did not know everything and I did not want to.

I did not want to know what happened to Barbara.

I did not want to know what was happening in the basement the day all the senior staff were summoned there and, as Senior Control, I was left in charge. Next came the Old Man's voice over the radio.

"Send Maureen down."

Maureen's face looked pale and shocked at the sound of her name. Maureen wore sweaters, cardigans with flowers and blue cable-knit pullovers. Even after six months at NOC, Maureen didn't smoke and she didn't swear. She told me that her father slapped her face when she told him she was calling off her wedding to join the organization, and it didn't sound like that was the first time he'd hit her. She was recruited so quickly and easily that the field office where she started out was worried she was a cop. But the Old Man had a theory that agents didn't last too long at NOC. "Nobody works this hard for a fuckin' salary," he said.

"Bring legal pads and pens," the Old Man shouted over the radio.

Shorthand, that's why he was calling her. She'd gone to secretary school. Maureen's face softened a little.

In this house where many of the women began to bleed on the same day, I could see that we were each caught in our separate revolutions. Nicole had lived at NOC for five years, and had not talked to the Old Man once in the time I'd been there. Maureen with her prim plump body might have been the same way, except for shorthand. Watching Maureen go, I thought about how we fell into the centre of things because of our interesting histories, our useful hands.

203

The thing in the basement went on for days. What were they doing down there? I didn't know. A trial of some kind, I thought. The punishment for defection in the military was death. Had anyone ever actually been killed for leaving? It could have been a court martial. I didn't want to know. But I did know what Maureen was doing: she was writing it all down.

Writing it down. I'd started writing it down too. Not all of it, but what I could: dreams, poems, fragments of conversation, thoughts I could not shake, words to pop songs I didn't know if I was remembering or writing.

I'm a practical girl in a practical world, but it's practically all over now.

For Christmas that year my mother sent me a photocopied version of the family photo album she'd been putting together at her parents' house in Seattle. In one photo, my grandfather, young and overexposed in the Xerox, stands in a line of men wearing fedoras, each one proudly holding a fish. All the men in the photograph are preachers like him, men who quoted the Bible and promised heaven and hell at revivals and on Indian reserves and in the poorest parts of town. Maybe I was born to it, a dissatisfaction bred into the bone with the world as it was. Like my mother, like her father and his father before him: a darkness inside we wanted to fill with something radiant. And yet despite everything, they'd all had trouble being true believers. My grandfather left the Nazarenes and his family, losing years to a gambling addiction. Even before my mother went AWOL from the Church and the Party, there had been a family history of broken faith and sudden departures.

With less than two months to go in the countdown, my mother's present, bulky and sentimental, made me wonder what she and others in the field had ever been told about the deadline. The closer we came, the more difficult it was to imagine. Maybe when the revolution started, we would all go into hiding, go into full combat mode. There had to be part of the plan the Old Man hadn't revealed and, like the sound of his voice, I longed and dreaded to hear it.

In my journal I write:

He once told me—watch out for the third purge,
Sonja. The 1st and 2nd will pass you by but watch out
for the third. The third purge is of idealism.

Looking at me behind my Control desk, it might have looked like I was working on a list or a memo. But really I was writing again.

What had the Old Man meant by that? That I would always want more, that I would never be satisfied?

On the next page I'd written down a line from a song I heard while I was down in the basement

205

courtyard. Looking up to see which window the song was coming from, I saw the octagon of brick-framed sky above me, cold and clear.

You can't walk in your sleep if you can't sleep, the song said.

Sometimes I felt like I was sleepwalking. Sometimes I felt like I couldn't sleep at all. Like the Old Man's words, I didn't fully understand it, but I wrote it down anyway so I wouldn't forget.

Midnight, and I was sitting at the watch desk scanning the street. When Polly told me I was on night watch I'd been surprised but not unhappy. Maybe the Old Man would call for me. I'd spent whole shifts in the Old Man's office. And if he didn't call, maybe that was okay too. Sitting almost alone with my notebook.

But I soon understood why Polly had wanted me on the desk.

On the watch log I wrote, *All quiet.*

And in my journal I wrote, *The neighbour is beating his wife again.*

Not even in my diary could I tell myself the truth.

The neighbour beats his wife and I can hear it through the radiator pipe. God how I wish the punks would be loud on the stoop again, but it is too cold, and I stare out the window and listen.

Struggler getting beat up that night was a different sound than Polly's soft whimper, the slap of flesh, the complicated intimate noises that slipped through the gap under the door when Polly got the whip. Struggler's cries rose up from the floor below, she wailed, she was frantic when he beat her. The crash of falling furniture in the Old Man's office, and the sound of her voice, keening like an animal. Sometimes I heard the Old Man's voice, too, but I suspected there was someone else too, someone holding her, or maybe hitting her on his behalf. Polly? Mary T? Maybe both. In less than two months, the revolution was scheduled to begin. I looked at the shadows of branches on the street, at every suspicious face or car that went by. I listened, but the only thing I heard was Struggler's voice crying *no, no, no.*

By my nineteenth birthday in the spring, I knew all this would be over. One way or another, it would all be different.

A few weeks later I was on night watch again. Someone new was working the Control desk in the morning, sleeping on my couch. She only worked a few days a week at the desk. The Old Man wanted me available to work on a special project. Word of this project was delivered to me from other people's conversations with him, but already Mary T was training people on the

207

Control desk. The new project had to do with creating training programs. While I waited for clearer orders I helped out with night watch and other duties and watched the days get changed on the countdown. It seemed late to be starting training programs. Mary T talked about the project like it was a promotion but that almost made it worse. This next thing did not sound as real or even as important as what I was giving up: my desk and my couch, my voice on the radio and my presence in the centre of things.

"Who's up there?" he called over the CB radio. Outside it was starting to get light.

"It's me," I said. "Sonja." Had the Old Man ever said my name?

He told me to bring him down a pot of coffee. He was smiling when I walked into his office.

"I've been wanting to talk to you. Sit down. I've got a story to tell you."

Dialectics was the truth that inside each thing was the force drawing everything towards its opposite. That's what Pat told me. "Shut up, shut up," she'd screamed in the Old Man's face, her hands clenched in shaking fists, the veins in her neck standing out like bones.

Dialectics said that there was a connection between the quantity and quality of things too. A single grain of rice was still rice, but we needed lots of rice for it to truly fulfill its purpose. Sand, snow, rain. I had come up with a dozen examples, and now I had learned even more.

A single lie, a dozen lies.

Hours that added up to years, that counted down to a single day.

Maybe dialectics could explain how I went from being that girl who thought she could see through everybody to the one who couldn't, who wouldn't, see what was right in front of her. All those signs. They should have added up to something. Something more than trembling hands and coded phrases in a diary.

The names of the women he fucked or beat, or promised to fuck, or threatened to beat.

The lies I had heard him tell, the pills I knew he took.

The pleading note from Struggler I'd found back when I still cleaned the Old Man's office. The note in the desk drawer was folded crookedly, into a small rectangle. Struggler's thin spidery writing, girlish even, on the lined paper, saying she couldn't stand it anymore. If the beatings didn't stop, she said. She'd do anything to make it stop. She'd kill herself. She'd take all the blame.

The note wasn't dated. Had Lisa found it too? How many other women did just what I did and fold the note back into each crease, placing it just so, so that no one would know it had been touched? So we could all pretend it hadn't been seen.

The beatings didn't stop. Another sign.

But in the end, I didn't need any signs at all. Because he told me. He told me it was all a lie.

He said: "Close your eyes and imagine it's February eighteenth. It's morning, and the sun is shining, and everyone is waiting. They are all waiting for the revolution to begin. And they wait. And then it's late morning. And I call you on the radio. And you come down here, and I'm lying on the couch, and I tell you I want chicken soup. I tell you I'm not feeling well. And then it's afternoon, and a lot of the cadre have left. I can hear them, walking out the door. Some of them are crying.

"And I call you down here on the radio again. And I tell you I want more soup."

I could picture the day he was talking about. It was a day like today, a day like yesterday. A morning just like this one, a morning that was fading into an afternoon, that was fading into another day I couldn't get back again. Sixteen days from now. I knew I had to stay, if only to see what happened at the end of the story. Maybe instead of leading a revolution the Old Man would choose me to go out to Montauk Point with him. He'd talked about that a few times before. Taking a drive out to someplace pretty, just us and the silver .45, leaving this corrupt world behind. And despite everything I knew and everything I suspected, I thought I would still say yes.

Because I did not know how to say no to him.

Because what I wanted, what the Old Man wanted, was to be important, to be the catalyst, the hero. But I could see that neither of us was going to get that, and neither of us knew what to do about it. And suddenly I felt like I had known this for a long time already.

"I'd bring you the soup." I said. "But it would be cold."

"I know," he said. "I know you'd bring me soup."

The sun was getting stronger through the slats in the window. I lit the Old Man another cigarette, and one for me, and stared at the landscape painting on the wall and that tiny square of shadow and light where everything worked.

"I have a story for you," I said. "Russian peasants discover that their wheat is bad, that eating it is going to drive them crazy. So they appoint a committee to watch over them, and give the committee the small supply of uncontaminated wheat. And it all works fine until the townspeople decide that the committee is crazy, and kill them."

"What's your point?" the Old Man said.

"I don't know." It was four a.m. Who were the townspeople in our story, who was the committee? Maybe we were all the wheat. "It's just a story I heard."

He said that was a story from World War II. There was another one about an army commander who told his troops that every time they'd lost, he'd heard a

211

strange laugh. The next battle, the troops hear the laugh and as they're being captured and taken prisoner, they see that it's their commander, laughing at them.

For years there has been a rumour, apparently spread by saboteurs in left-wing media, that the organization was a government front. I had never seen these accusations and how exactly that would work had never been clear to me. Could the Old Man be saying this was true? We sat in silence for a while.

Finally I said, "If I really believed that's what was going to happen on the eighteenth, I don't know what I'd still be doing here. Why wait? Why stay?" I started to cry.

"I don't know," he said. "I don't know what you're doing here. Leave. You can leave right now if you want to."

That's what he said. But I'd learned that words weren't reliable, words shifted tense and ownership and intent too easily. Can for should, will for might. I already knew that about words, and about people too. Instead I looked at body language, I looked at recent events. And I didn't think the Old Man was really going to let me walk out that door.

I didn't think I wanted to be caught, halfway through that door.

TWENTY-TWO

Nine days before the revolution was supposed to begin we woke up to Harold, sitting behind the Ops desk where Struggler usually sat. Harold was a tall black man who had the stillness and powers of concentration of someone used to confined spaces (and it won't surprise me, years later, to learn that he'd been an escaped prisoner, convicted of murder). As part of my own training, I'd sat in on many of Harold's recruitment briefings when he'd come from a field office a year earlier. I felt some pride in how, after only a year, he was authentic to the revolution in a way that many of us knew we could never be.

Harold told us he had orders from the Old Man. We were taking a day to regroup. We weren't allowed to work. We weren't allowed to do anything except sit and think about what the fuck we were doing. By noon, we were all still sitting in the meeting room, where we usually held the morning briefing, some of us spilling into the kitchen and hallway. I was grateful to be sitting at the Control desk instead of stuck, like some of the others, sitting on the floor.

Watching Harold, with his booming voice and balled-up fists as he read from the pronouncements the Old Man had given him, I felt certain that the Old Man hadn't told him the same story he'd told me. Since talking to the Old Man, I'd been watching the faces of the Central Committee members, listening for whispers of dissent and anger. The worry sore that Struggler had on the crown of her head, the place she rubbed at when anxious, was raw and Polly looked like she had the flu. They knew. But not Harold.

We spent the morning dozing and reading anything that happened to be near us—until these activities were also declared unacceptable. We raised our hand for permission to go to the bathroom. Harold went between the meeting room and the Old Man's office, his heavy footsteps on the stairs the loudest sound we heard for hours.

At five o'clock the Old Man went to sleep, and Harold suddenly thought about dinner, which was usually an all-day job.

Harold shouted: "Who's gonna cook this mother-fuckin' dinner?"

Finally he picked Mary T and Polly.

"Everybody fucking cooks. No shit jobs in the revolution, people. Everybody fucking cooks."

But, of course, he was wrong.

Harold was wrong and now he had to be killed. That's what the Old Man was shouting the next morning, shouting in Struggler's face as he leaned into her face, his gimpy foot lifting off the floor. He's going to fall on her, I thought. He told Struggler he had to kill Harold and it was her fault. She'd let him question her authority; she'd allowed him to challenge the position of the Party's leadership.

"Now he's got to go and it's all your fucking fault."

Struggler's pale blue eyes were big as she worked to understand what he was saying.

"But Oldie . . ." she said. Oldie was her special name for him, almost no one else called him that. Was she going to point out the obvious, that the Old Man put him in charge, that no one really believed Struggler was the Party's leader? And then, as though at the same moment Struggler and I realized the

215

same thing: it didn't matter what she said. She stopped talking.

"All your fucking fault," the Old Man yelled.

I was standing at the doorway holding the Old Man's breakfast tray. I could feel my legs starting to shake. I'd been up all night on watch duty again. A few hours ago I'd been watching the sun come up and writing in my diary.

I am sitting at a window 3 and a half hours now, I am watching a street I rarely walk along.

Shortly after that he called me down to his office and I'd spent the rest of the night delivering coffee and cigarettes and food. I'd fallen asleep on his couch sometime after the sun came up and when he woke me he gave me a big orange pill. "Stay with me, kid."

Now the pill was looking for places to go in my blood, banging on my heart like someone trying to get out. I was used to taking Sudafed for my bronchitis and also to keep me awake, sometimes five or six in a day. But this was the first time I'd had one of the Old Man's pills. At about 8:30 he'd sent me to make him scrambled eggs and bacon, and when I came back, he was telling Struggler they had to kill Harold. The quiet hours I'd spent watching the window before this all began felt like a lifetime ago, like it happened to someone else completely.

I could see the light in Struggler's eyes change. They'd been filled with something. Doubt. Uncertainty. Panic. Concern for Harold. Suddenly all that was gone, and what was left was emptiness, metallic and flat. Outside, the snow and clouds were making the sky shift in the windows, a luminescent grey. Inside, Mary's eyes went their palest blue as she gave up.

"Just tell me what you need me to do, Oldie."

"Whatever you say, Oldie."

I spent all day in and out of the Old Man's office, watching the molecules of air shimmer and waiting for someone to kill Harold. Every time I drifted off to sleep the Old Man gave me another pill. He got me to make him lunch, canned chili with saltines stacked neatly around the rim while he made phone calls on his private line. This was the first time I'd spent with him since he told me the story, the chicken soup story, he called it at the time. Now he acted like that whole conversation had never happened.

I was on the third or fourth pill by the time I sat down next to the Old Man at the folding table for class night, the first and only time he'd ever ask me to sit beside him. The air was a television screen made up of tiny points of light that shifted between static and perfect focus. Struggler staring straight ahead. Harold looking like a man straining to overhear a conversation. He knew something was wrong, but he didn't know the something was him.

When the Old Man picked up a cigarette, I lit it for him with his brass Zippo, the one with the Airborne logo engraved on it.

The Old Man said when you jumped from a parachute, there was a moment where you were no longer falling towards the ground, but, instead, the earth was rising up at you. I thought about the look in Struggler's eyes, how that was another trick of light, an optical illusion. To watch the blue of someone's eye change from the soft blue of concern and confusion to icy clarity and determination. The clarity of knowing that giving in was the only way out. The determination that whatever was going to happen, it wouldn't happen to her.

The Old Man said that the ground rose up to meet you, and you were caught, motionless in space. That's what it felt like, just before you hit the ground. I knew it was just a shift in perspective, that it wasn't real. But I was approaching this moment. I could feel it in every cell in my body.

The day before the revolution the men in uniform came across the back courtyard wall, and on the roof. They came down the street. They came, as though in slow motion, or maybe it was only lack of sleep that took the speed out of things, that made everything seem unhurried and inevitable. If we'd had a plan, something we knew we were supposed to do, we might have panicked, trying to carry it out. Instead most of us just sat and waited for them to come through the doors.

Except the front watch, who shouted, "They're here, they're here."

And the Old Man, who screamed as he fell down the dumbwaiter, trying to escape.

We were all in the courtyard, huddled against the cold. It reminded me a little of fire drills at school, the sunlight and the sudden giddy surprise of finding yourself outside.

"We're all lost," Lilia said. Lilia was standing beside me. Like many of us, she was dressed in a donated janitor uniform, the men's extra large, the shirt hanging down to just above the knees, but she still smelled like soap and cinnamon, like she had the first day I met her. A shampoo maybe, or a cologne, something she'd hung on to in all the time she'd been here.

We'd been standing outside for hours already, watching as plaster dust plumed through the open windows of the apartments into the February air. Inside, the FBI and city police were tearing out the walls of the two suites we used most. They'd begun bringing boxes out of the house. Clothes, papers, a box of shoes—there seemed to be no logic to what they carried away. At our request, and after looking them over, they'd brought us out our boxes of bedding, cigarettes and socks. Some of us wore the socks as mittens.

I was watching the police officers, standing shoulder to shoulder, relaxed but with the clubs still in their hands.

Lilia said, "Without the Old Man we don't know what to do. Our own training manual says every organizer should be replaceable. But look at us. This is not how it's supposed to be. This is classic charismatic leadership."

I looked around. I could see how pale we all were, compared to the cops and the FBI and the curious neighbours. It occurred to me that this was the first time I'd seen many of these faces in natural light. We looked like refugees, displaced people, in our blanket coats and our grey janitor clothes.

"Shut up," I said to her and walked away. How could she say this when we were surrounded by cops? When the Old Man was hurt, and the cops wouldn't let anyone see him?

Still, even I wondered why we hadn't at least practised the dumbwaiter. If that was the plan, shouldn't we have tried it out first? Why didn't I know about it?

The dumbwaiter hadn't held his weight, and he'd fallen down the shaft and broken his leg. Which one? No one was sure yet. He was in the doctor's office with the police and the ambulance attendants.

By afternoon we were still standing in the courtyard.

Someone started to sing. We started with "This Land Is Your Land," and we went on from there.

We sang so the Old Man could hear us, so he would know we were waiting for him. We sang because it was something for us to do, and now that the fear had worn off, the boredom had set in. I sang because I didn't want to think. I didn't want to think about the story that the Old Man told me, or about the phone calls he'd been making, or about how the cops didn't really seem very interested in us. They asked us if we were being held against our will, if anyone of us wanted to leave, but they didn't ask for our names. I sang because I didn't want to think about whether Lilia was right, and maybe neither did she, because when I looked over, she was singing too.

We sang labour songs and gospel and folk and when we sang "Yankee Doodle Dandy," the cops applauded. At the beginning of the winter there were eighty-four of us. Now there were sixty-three. I caught a glimpse of someone's grey shirt, as he pushed his way to the edge of the crowd and down the street.

Sixty-two.

We were down to the true believers. Nothing had happened that was supposed to happen. And yet still we stood in the cold and waited for the Old Man to tell us what to do.

221

———

When they finally let us back inside we kept finding new things missing. The CB radios from the Control desk and the other stations, pictures of Lenin taken off the walls. My book of radio codes was gone. The small closet room, the Cave, which the Old Man sometimes used as a sleeping room, had been searched from top to bottom. The FBI found only a few weapons, old and not very useful. I was not surprised, since some things had been moved the week before. Where, how? I only knew the sounds of heavy lifting I'd heard from the office, the absence of the guns in the room. It seemed strange to me that there was a plan for the guns, but not for the dumbwaiter escape. This mystery was its own distraction. But still there were basic things to be done. Coffee to be made. Dinner to be cooked. Cigarettes to be smoked, and the street to watch in case they came back.

A week after the raid I was on night watch again. The cops were more obvious now: vans parked across the street, men with binoculars at the window. What was I watching them for? The watch couldn't keep them out. It could barely keep us in.

In my journal I wrote,

The silence of early morning watch shifts and the emergence of spring outside the window is almost painful to me. A dangerous melancholy. Everything changed but nothing changed. Just like he told me it would.

Since his fall down the dumbwaiter, the Old Man lived in the haze of new drugs that the ex-medical student got for him by forging the AWOL doctors' names.

But even with eyes like pinpricks, the Old Man was still in charge. He shouted out new orders, about newsletters and calls to action and lawsuits. With his freshly busted-up leg, he needed more help than he ever did before, so I was called upon to do things like carry a fresh needle or new bandages from the doctor's office one apartment over.

Hurrying through the basement hallways and courtyards I found myself rhyming my thoughts into lyrics of something that was almost a song:

Running through a burning corridor
I am just a wooden soldier for
a war of fire
tender wood
would tender words
bring a flood
to fight the flame and
ashen blood
to cure the lame
(break a leg again)

223

And once the song is in my head I can't get it out, even as I'm handing Polly his bandages, even as I'm asking him how he's feeling.

———

I brought the bandages, I brought the needles, I brought the protein shakes and the cigarettes and the coffee that he needed. And with these things I brought those big eyes he'd teased me about, full of panic, not all of it for him.

He must have seen that, seen it and not liked it, because one night when I was back at the Control desk he took over my housing logistics, re-arranging all of the people and all of the cars, confusing me so much I started to shout, "That won't work, it just won't work!"

Even as I said it, I felt the dangerous pleasure Pat must have known when she shouted at the Old Man to shut the fuck up. Tanya's grandmother slapped me across the face, telling me to stop being so hysterical, and just as her hand struck my skin I understood that I'd been set up, that this had been what he wanted all along. All night I kept touching the warmth of my cheek even after it was gone. This was what it felt like. This was the line I'd crossed over. And once you were over you couldn't go back.

The countdown numbers, like the pictures of Lenin, were gone from the wall, taken by the FBI. Nicotine stains on the wall framed everything that was missing. Our new radio didn't have very strong reception so the voices I'd gotten to know on the CB were gone and I missed the truckers and cabbies whose conversations

I'd listened to when I slept by the radio at night. Ten days after the revolution was supposed to begin, John came to the Control desk and handed me a notebook, a hardcover composition books with "School Days" on the cover. "Maybe you'll get better use out of this than I have."

Inside he'd written one entry, at the beginning of February.

> Started the last days—if this thing is as historic as
> everybody says it is supposed to be theoretically then
> we might as well record history . . . I will write what I
> can and what I have patience to at the end of each day
> which is getting to be more like closer to the start . . .

The last days. Where were we now? At the start? At the end? Since the raid I couldn't tell.

In my new journal I wrote about the strangers from the radio.

> Today would have been a good day to listen. Clear
> skies. Strange that I should miss them.

I watched the back window, my eyes shifting from the sun on the courtyard to my own reflection. I was going to be nineteen soon. I felt a small flutter of panic, like I did when I'd taken too many pills.

225

Maureen put in her resignation to the Central Committee. She was doing it by the books, the first time I'd ever seen someone try that. In the meantime she said she'd do only non-political work. Dishes. Cooking. She cleaned toilets, she swept floors, and so for the Control Officer, she was a kind of blessing, a set of free hands for every occasion, although it had been days since I'd heard her speak. Maybe she was a cop after all. Maureen was putting something to the test. Was it that she could leave the right way, by fighting it out, by making her point? Or was it that even this was a lie, this elaborate bureaucracy, the constitution in its leather binder? As I watched her silently working I wondered if Maureen was brave, or stupid, or protected. I could not risk believing I was any of those things.

A month after the raid I gave John a note with his nightly logistics.

I had a friend once who left without saying goodbye and I never quite forgave her.

In the five minutes it took me to walk there, I would know whether I was going to try to get to the train or the tracks of the Carroll Street subway station around the corner. All I needed was five minutes. Or an hour. A day to think things through. I wrote down my father's number in the note.

John called NOC an hour later, and said he had a question about his logistics. When I got on the phone he asked me if I was going to Long Island, and I said no.

"Well, what is this number then? It's a Long Island area code."

"No," I said. "That's a mistake." And it was, because I'd written the area code wrong.

But he didn't tell anyone. Was his silence indifference or a gift? He'd given me candy and a nickname and the most delicate of kisses on the stairway at midnight. It wasn't much, but it was something. Something else I'd have to leave behind.

In the basement, my dog emerged from the furnace room, just as I came out of the communal cubbyspace. I'd taken all the change I could find out of everyone's pockets, and it added up to less than five dollars. She stood in the hallway, wagging her tail. I squatted down and put my arms around her. My sweet Gemini who stood and wagged her tail while a bully broke my nose when I was thirteen. And yet still I'd insisted on taking her wherever I moved, from Redding to Montreal to New York. I'd insisted on pretending that we were capable of protecting each other. Little girls and dogs, with our helpless, endless love.

If I didn't go now, I didn't know when I'd have another chance. Just after Tanya had woken me up for morning watch she was called down to the Old Man's office. Was he fucking her right now? Most likely he was talking about fucking her someday, somewhere. Not here, and not now. Today he was impotent and strung-out. The Old Man had even less to offer Tanya than he did to me. But he could still promise. Promise he was going to fuck her brains out, or love her forever.

Polly, Mary T, Beth, Jayne, Susan, Linda. Others I never even noticed. Now Tanya. Who the Old Man had on the couch today was a question I tried not to ask anymore, an answer I didn't need to know.

Except today.

Today I needed to figure how long she was going to be in there, how long it was likely to take. Today his attraction to her was an unexpected opportunity, a gift I couldn't afford to refuse.

The day before I'd written in my journal,

So here it is Monday. I am nineteen today and that is nothing, nothing at all.

Later on that evening he called me down to his office. He said, "Is something on your mind, little girl?" Something had been reported to him. An expression on my face, or maybe reports of crying in the bathroom.

"It's my birthday," I said.

He said, "I know. I know that, you think I don't know that? Happy Birthday," he said, gesturing towards the bourbon bottle. Within a few minutes he'd drifted off to sleep.

But here was my real present: calling little Tanya down to his office, choosing her instead of me. Even as I was telling Gemini that I loved her, as I was telling her I was sorry, whispering into her velvety ears, I was listening for footsteps on the stairs. I hadn't thought at all about leaving my dog, because if I thought about it, if I'd pictured this moment once in my mind, I'd have to stay forever. If I thought about what the Old Man might do, or threaten to do, just to keep me or punish me or both, I'd have to stay forever. I could only save one of us, and only if I hurried.

Later is when I'd cry. Later I could have anything I wanted, I told myself. I could have the third rail or I could have a thousand more days to forgive this moment and decide what to do with my life. But at that moment all I had was the unwatched street.

PART FOUR

The question whether objective truth can be
attributed to human thinking is not a question
of theory but is a practical question.

KARL MARX, "THESES ON FEUERBACH,"
THESIS 2 (1845)

TWENTY-THREE

After the revolution, my mother said, things would be different. And they were.

After the revolution, right after, all I had were nightmares and daydreams and one canvas bag that contained everything that was left of the girl I'd been before. Dialectics said that everything contained the potential for its opposite. Like the tears to laughter and back again when days after I left, Susan called me at my father's house and asked, "Is it because he missed your birthday? Is that why you left?" The fact that he had gotten Susan of the red pubic hair in the Vaseline, to call me, showed how little he knew me. Polly was my measure of things, the one I looked to see the girl I was, the woman I might become.

"We didn't win," I said. "Nothing happened."

"Why do you say that?"

"Because. Because I was there."

I was there, I saw. I had to keep reminding myself of this. Even if I didn't know everything, I knew enough. Even if I was wrong and the Old Man hadn't called for the raid, he'd beaten Polly with a crop, he'd beaten Mary T and Struggler, and the day after the revolution, nothing was different. I wanted to hear how Susan would justify it but I could tell that Susan, answering everything I said with a question, didn't really know yet. It had been over a month and not even the Old Man had been able to come up with a way to explain exactly what really had gone down.

Sometimes I wondered what the Old Man thought would happen when he went for the dumbwaiter, what part of the plan went wrong? And then I thought back to the day he told me the chicken soup story and wondered if there had ever been any plan at all. Working all the angles was not the same thing as a plan.

———

Dialectics said history worked in spirals not circles—
we could never have the same day over again, we could
never go back to the place we started—but we could
come deceptively close. And so I found myself walking
down familiar streets with the same wonder I'd had
when I first moved to Montreal as a little
girl, the same amazement at how many
separate worlds could live side by side, how
many words there could be for any one
thing. And how many things couldn't be
translated at all.

On the phone my mother tried to comfort me with Lenin's words that not everyone was cut out to be cadre, but that didn't
mean we had to stand in the way of the
others who carried on. In my father's
house I stayed in the mustard yellow guest
room, because my old bedroom was now the nursery.
At mealtimes we talked about the weather and the
crossword and all the things his new baby son was
learning. My sister called and said it was about time I
came to my senses. "That guy was so crazy," she said.

The first job I got on the outside was as a telephone
solicitor. Every morning the phone crew did the PMA
chant. Positive Mental Attitude spelled out like the
YMCA dance. Our job was to get people to come see
a presentation on summer timeshares. Later, it turned
out the whole thing was a scam.

235

A month into that job I got fired because my sales numbers were too low and I spent too long talking to old people. The next day I got a job as a waitress at a sports bar. I told them I had experience serving in New York and this did not seem like a lie.

I got my own apartment and enrolled as a mature student at the local college, paying for my tuition with money I got from my dad for holding his drug stash. I took a course called Knowledge and Human Nature. The textbook was heavier than the bag I'd taken with me from New York.

The first day of class I sat in the only left-handed desk in the room ready to take careful notes. Despite everything, I still wanted someone to tell me what was true, what was real. Our teacher wore a lavender dress made of shiny synthetic material and wobbled on her heels. Grey roots showed through her mink brown dyed hair, and there was a slight tremble to her hands. When she spoke her voice had a high singing quality to it. She stared out the window at the back of the classroom and said, "When we define truth, what exactly are we defining?"

How is truth defined? I wrote this down. I put a star beside this. I underlined this. I traced the ink lines of my words on the page. When I first went to Brooklyn, I wanted the red star tattoo that some of the old timers like Rena had. Sitting in the classroom I wanted it more than ever. I wanted some proof of where I'd been, proof it all happened. If not the truth, then at least this. Evidence. A testament to my faith, a scar to remember it by.

For the first few months after I got out I'd been amazed by how different the outside world was. But it didn't take long to start to see the similarities; the tiny ways people fell apart every day, trapped in lives they didn't believe in anymore. The tremble of the teacher's hand. The bored looks on the other students' faces.

The girl who smelled like baby powder, the last person to ask me not to go to New York, was also one of the few people I saw when I came back. "I'm here to steal your girlfriend," I told the man she'd been dating the first time we all went out together for a drive in his BMW. He might have been relieved—he was nineteen and they'd recently gotten engaged. But did she want to be stolen? That wasn't entirely clear. She wanted to bring me food when I ran out. She wanted to pat my back when I cried and she didn't want to ask questions. She wanted to kiss me when she was drunk. Those things were good enough for me.

And worth paying for, which is what it felt like I was doing the night the boyfriend woke me up to have sex. When I tell her she cries but doesn't call it off with either of us. We even try with the three of us together, but it was a failure of geometry and coordination. And none of us really wanted to share.

Sex was what I did instead of apologizing, instead of small talk. I had little patience for listening to people

237

talk about their meaningless lives and talking about myself was worse. Explaining why I didn't know who Boy George was or that Darth Vader was Luke's father. I interrupt a nice young man mid conversation to tell him that I'm actually a bit bored but we could fuck if he wants to, I live just around the corner. I even had sex with the little dealer again for some cocaine and a chance to get in on his next deal. In bed I tried to imagine myself as a drug dealer—the clothes I'd wear, leather and heels, the things I'd say. Later, cutting lines, I realized I wasn't strong enough to carve off a piece of myself like that. But I wasn't weak enough to let just anyone else do it either. Even if I did need someone to take the Old Man's place I'd have to look a little harder. There were days when I couldn't believe I was never going to talk to him again and nights when I couldn't get his voice out of my head, *pretty, pretty girl*. He had transformed me in ways I was still discovering.

Everywhere, melodies, lyrics and drum lines shouted at me from the dance floor, the radio, leaking from the headphones of fellow passengers on the bus. Pop songs by Eurythmics and Elton John reminding me how human, how normal, it was to be sad. What were other people sad about? I couldn't imagine.

In my apartment, with my own lock and key and my father's big navy steamer trunk full of drugs in my living room, I was sometimes the centre of too much attention but often alone. No one cared when I walked out my front door, where I was going, when I'd be back. Sometimes this was exhilarating but other days it was terrifying to think that I could just let myself disappear. I got a cat just to make sure I had a reason to go home.

Some days I could count the many pleasures of my new life: the cat purring on my bed, this window that opened and closed, the view of the park, these books, this drink, this stranger, this body that I lived in with no one to tell me how or when to use it. This self that didn't want to die, that didn't stay in Brooklyn, that didn't throw herself on the tracks, that didn't want to waste any more time.

And other days I made this same list, all the things I would give away, just to believe in something again. Just for that radiant certainty. The revolution I'd counted down to had been like the sun, so bright it lit every corner of my life, and yet I could not look directly at it. Couldn't. Wouldn't. It ended up the same in the end. The doubts I didn't let myself feel, the words I didn't write.

It was the other waitress on my Saturday shift at the restaurant who first used the word "cult." She was a poli-sci student at McGill. Maybe that's how the subject came up.

"Oh no," I said. "It was political."

"You should look up the definition of cult," the poli-sci waitress said. "Because I am telling you, that's what it sounds like."

239

TWENTY-FOUR

I'm sitting in the dark in front of my computer. The lights are off because it is late at night and what I am doing feels secret. My fingers on the keyboard are light and shaky. I hit the return key and there he is.

He is dead.

The first *New York Times* obituary of Eugenio Perente-Ramos is dated March 20, 1995, and calls him an organizer of migrant and seasonal labourers and a close associate of Cesar Chavez in the United Farm Workers Organizing Committee. The next day, a correction, seven paragraphs long, names him Gerald

Doeden, "the leader of a group that has been charac-
terized as a cult."

I find a website called "The Truth About
NATLFED." There are the obituaries, and a photo of
his tombstone. I cry when I see the portrait on it. His
thin face, the bandana at his neck. In one of my dreams
about the Old Man he looked just like that. In that
dream I am crying at his graveside and, gradually, I
realize the coffin is surrounded by women, all of us
weeping in our black dresses. I could see us as a group
for the first time. Me and Jayne and Beth and Linda
and Polly and Mary and Susan and Tanya, and others
standing just outside of my view. And then the Old
Man showed up looking younger and healthier than
I'd ever seen him. He was laughing at us. And we were
so relieved to see him we didn't care.

This is the only photo I've ever seen of him and even
that is a lie.

World class revolutionary fighter

Internationalist soldier

Son of the American working class

Theologian, philosopher, historian

Teacher, writer, broadcaster, machinist

Farm worker, labor and community organizer

Gentleman and friend

Beloved comrade

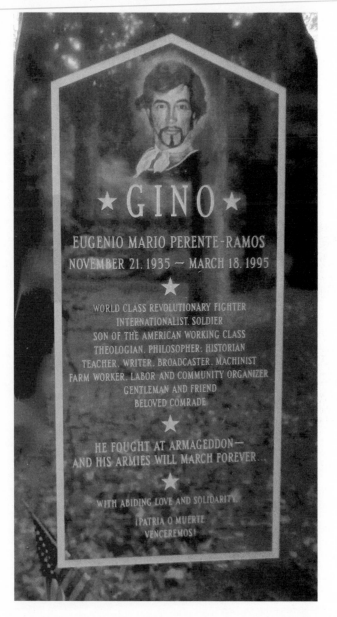

I wondered if he wrote the epitaph himself, except I don't think even he would have described himself as a gentleman or a friend. Of all the lies on the stone I find the part about "son of the American working class" the most puzzling, since he often described himself as the son of Mexican wetbacks. Maybe the stone came after the corrected obituary when he's revealed not to be Mexican at all, but distantly Norwegian, just like me.

For years after the revolution I was either struggling to remember or pretending that none of it ever happened. One of the best places to do either was on the dance floor. There were moments when I was dancing that the beat seemed to break apart everything I knew, and under a strobe light I could see how he used me. Like an X-ray showing me all my broken places.

On the dance floor was where I met my first husband at twenty, and where I mourned our divorce at twenty-four. I loved his easy rhythm, tidy apartment, the easy way he cooked us meals, brought me to orgasm for the very first time. We met because we were the only two dancing to a complicated Smiths song. At the end of the night he asked if I wanted to go home with him. "I'm here with someone," I said. "But don't cross me off your list."

He did not cross me off his list.

Another part of what I loved about him was what a good recruit he'd have been. How hungry he was for all the things the revolution could have given him. He was

reading Ayn Rand when we met and so I read her, too, talking him out of every point. I could not really imagine either of us getting old. We moved in together after a month. He said he loved me. He said love should be a rational agreement between people. He said he didn't believe in happily ever after. *We should get married,* he said to me. *You could get a bigger student loan then.* And when I found out my permanent resident status was being reviewed, we set a date.

Walking down the stairs of my father's house, I know that even though this is the only thing I know how to do, it's a mistake. A mistake to think I can be given away, or keep a promise that big. I've failed before, I'll fail again.

And of course I do.

After our separation I went to see a therapist but it didn't last too long. She took too many notes, she sketched a diagram, she wanted it all right from the start. We barely talk about my separation, instead she kept coming back, over and over again, to the hitch-hiking trip and after the fourth session I realize that, even with the discount she's giving me, I can't afford to answer the questions she's asking me. So I quit.

The first man I sleep with after my husband is an astrologist. He makes my chart. He gives me an STD and the observation that, from the placement of the moon in my chart, I am the kind of person who understands the world through metaphor.

"No shit," I say.

At university I kept finding new ways to think and not to think about my life. I thought about the Old Man's whip during a lecture about Marshall McLuhan and how the medium is the message. When I read Foucault's ideas about the ways power is created and consolidated through accepted forms of knowledge, it sent a shiver through me. The messages we sent and received without words. How no one, not the bus driver, not Karl not the Old Man, had to tell me to keep a secret. Our shared understanding of the accepted forms of knowledge.

And eventually I follow the advice that the poli-sci waitress gave me. I look it up. I give it that name. Cult. High-demand group.

The sense of urgency. The time table. The secret language. The mythical elements. The sexual control. The lack of sleep. The control, internal and external, over thought and movement. The denial of self.

245

There was a checklist, and I made a mark by nearly every line.

The naming is both liberating and shameful. It gave me the language to share my experience. And the more I read the more I understood that if the Old Man was a checklist then I was too.

Historian, his gravestone reads. A man like that can take away your history. He can give you a new one, if you let him. If you do not say no. For the first year this is all I do in my dreams: try and tell the Old Man no. After that it is often all I can say, in sporadic recurring nightmares where I return and am trapped again. No. But he never listens.

Historian. And teacher, I can't deny those titles. In the years I spent with him he taught me not to talk back, not to question anyone but myself. He taught me how to serve him dinner and say the things he wanted me to say. But before he did any of these things, he taught me that I was not too small to hold the gun, that would never be my excuse for whatever happened to me. That was something I needed to learn.

And because I was not only his student but a teacher's pet, I have that schoolbag of memories: the birthday card, the letters from my mother, my father, Karl and Dana. If he had not asked to see them, they would have stayed locked up with the rest of my things, the journals of my childhood, my teddy bear, my dog. Even if he only showed me how to survive his own fantasies and only gave back a few of the things that he took away, even if he did these things only by accident, by chance, that was still something. That was still more than others got.

More than Dana, whose teacher taught her to hold still for the rifle.

More than Polly, who died of cancer years before the Old Man. I'd heard, third-hand, a story of her sitting at class time with an oxygen mask over her face. That face I'd watched like a compass looking for some direction, a sign it was time to go. How did he feel not being the sickest person in the room, watching her escape right before his very eyes? More than Struggler, who I was told got out but never got free, and died in a fire a few years after she left.

Beloved comrade, the stone says. No one could deny that.

In the darkness I stare at the glowing monitor and let all of his lies and his smooth face shine back on me.

"I know you," I said the first time I met him. He was forty-six and looked older than he should have. I was sixteen and younger than I knew. That moment I would remember and forget over and over again in the years to come. That dialectical moment of doubt and certainty, that flickering instant between us in the low light of his office, the two of us with our dyed

247

black hair and our pale Nordic skin. How Gerald Doeden laughed when he said, "Of course you do. You're sixteen, you think you know everything." How he looked at me when he said, "I know you too."

The last time I saw Gerald Doeden I watched him drift off to sleep, his eyes rolling back into his head in a morphine drift. I sat in the dark, drinking my birthday bourbon, listening to him breathe, waiting and wishing for the moment he would stop. I had been in Brooklyn nearly nine hundred days and this was just another one.

And by the next afternoon I was in a Manhattan park, waiting for Western Union money to come through so I could get a ticket back to Montreal. As I lay in the sun, outside for the first time since the raid, I could feel the warmth on my skin, the edges of my body against the grass. After the revolution I'd told myself things would be different, but they weren't. The revolution had come and gone, and all I knew for certain was that I couldn't keep waiting anymore, sitting in the corner of a room, moving us from here to there, keeping track of every day and every hour, waiting for something to change. And I didn't want to be lying on his green velvet couch either. Getting what was mine, wishing myself into his broken landscape, losing track of the difference between day and night. I couldn't be Control or #25 or that most generic of names, little girl.

"When I'm dead, little girl, you're going to be sorry you said these things to me," he told me when I'd accused him of being addicted to sex and pills. "Maybe," I said. "Probably." I had waited a long time to find out the answer.

"No," I say in the darkness. "No," I say to the real and not real picture of the real and not real man I gave so much of myself to. "I'm not sorry."

TWENTY-FIVE

We are waiting to cross the border.

Off the side of the highway the sun shines down on the water where it's broken up into thousands of fragments of light. The road ahead of us is long and lined with idling cars as we wait to cross the border. Kevin sighs. I'm sitting in the passenger seat staring out at the bay. I live in Vancouver now, in the rainy salty climate that will always remind me of Dana and my grandparents. And every time we drive this road I find myself wondering if this is the border where Dale and I crossed over in the bus. So much is lost: Dale's last name, how I ended up on the road with him, not to mention everything of my life before. I have a memory of water. I think it was here. I'm almost certain.

"I'm sure it's nothing," my mother said when she called earlier in the day, her voice small with fear at finding herself in the emergency room. We live two hours apart but in separate countries, which for a woman who sees the world through metaphor seems right. We are allies mostly, but there is a border. There are sides.

As I listen to her on the phone I have a held-breath quiet inside me that is its own memory, repeated and remembered, remembered and repeated. The first time I can remember it might have been the night my mother asked me if she should leave my father. But probably this instinct for stillness was with me long before that.

"It's just a flu. But I got pretty sick and the dog needs to be walked. It was kinda scary how bad I was feeling. But I think they're going to let me out this afternoon."

Soon emotion will flood into this emptiness. Anger, fear, love. In minutes or hours or maybe years this memory of numbness will be one of the things I let in. But not now. Now I am waiting to cross the border.

I put my hand on Kevin's and thank him for driving me to see my mother. He was the first man I ever held hands with before kissing and I was almost thirty years old when we met. In many ways I could not

251

make this journey without him. Because I have lived with him longer than I ever lived with any of my family and through him learned a loyalty and a tenderness my own family could not teach me. And also because I can't drive.

Not learning how to drive at the same age as most people is one consequence of my childhood. And maybe never making up for it later is another consequence still. When we were first married Kevin tried to teach me. During the second lesson, in a Home Depot parking lot, he said, "Sometimes you can't avoid killing something. It isn't always safe to swerve out of the way. You have to choose." I asked him if he'd ever killed anything. A squirrel and a cat that he knew of, and once there was something dark and doglike on a country road. And that was the end of the driving lesson.

In every way I am no longer that girl. That girl who thought she could kill things. That girl who said yes. Standing in line at the grocery store or sitting in the passenger seat of the car, I am not the girl who chose to kill Barbara. Most days I know this. We are all different people now. My mother is not the woman she was. The woman who believed she could change the world, the woman who called herself my comrade, my comrade who went AWOL. Time and circumstance and even biology have changed us. Even the cells in our bodies have been transformed, not once but many times.

And yet what to do with these memories? Memories that outlast love and family and faith. Waiting by the side of the road for someone to see me. A remembered craving for certainty, for something true and absolute, addictive as any drug. The sound of the Old Man's voice saying it would be the kindest thing. Those memories that extend all the way into muscle, into reflexes that are well intentioned but dangerous. Holding my breath and waiting. A difficulty saying no. A way of watching and forgetting all at the same time.

Reflexes and confidence and trust. Those were just a few of the things I was missing and not just behind the wheel. And maybe, like the exact location of a border crossing on a map, they were something I could never quite recover.

When we arrive in Bellingham, my mother is out of the emergency room and already feeling better, although still weak. Her small apartment is neat and clean and the walls are decorated with her carefully carved prints of birds and shoes and musical instruments, her celebration of everyday beauty, she says. I'm seized with an appreciation for her creativity, her orderliness, for the vitamins and supplements she takes, the long list of foods she's eliminated from her diet to improve her health. She has lived alone for a long time now. Kevin and I walk her dog, make dinner, and buy groceries

253

while she sleeps. When she wakes up she shows me her latest artwork: block prints on old books.

For years I was angry with my mother, and this anger made me unpredictable even to myself. I wanted her to feel this pain I was only beginning to measure. *I'm sorry,* she said, not once but many times. *If I could change it I would.* And one day it was like I heard those words for the very first time. Even if I could write the script there was nothing she could say that would change what happened.

Gone is gone as gone can be. This is so plain yet it's hard to see.

We work hard not to have these conversations anymore. We don't get drunk, we don't talk about the past, we don't ask questions. Instead we try to talk about little things that bring us joy: dogs and art we love and good deals at the thrift store.

It probably helps that I'm happier now too. That my marriage to an engineer and a builder has taught me how happiness is the product of thousands of tiny connections, like nails in wood. How the structure of things should be as simple as it could be, but no simpler. I take his love and all the metaphors he gives me with gratitude.

The three of us sit and drink tea. We pet our dogs. She reminds me that I've helped her pick both the dogs she's had, and both were good choices. She asks about work. I am an accidental youth worker and techie in the community centre of a poor neighbourhood. My work is filled with people who remind me of ones met in soup lines as a child, at the food bank. I don't think that's an accident. There must be a reason I've worked so long in a place where every day I face some echo of my past. Maybe I need to remember. Maybe I can't forget. In the end it's the same thing. Over the years I witness a dozen versions of the girl I was, variations on all the girls of my family. Dana, my sister, my mother, my aunt. These girls, and all the ways they stand with their arms outstretched for whatever they can reach. These girls so new to the age of reason.

I don't know how to change the world. I don't know if it can be changed the way I tried. But people's worlds change sometimes. I express this belief in the most banal of ways: remembering a name, finding a pencil, asking if everything is okay, even though I know that being asked is not the same as being brave enough to tell. These small inadequate gestures that make up my day and that will probably not be enough. It takes more than this. Maybe most of all it takes luck. That the stranger who picks you up by the side of the road lets you go. That you survive the dangerous men who can spot a girl like you and that Little Red Riding Hood target on your back. I know this. Yet there are days when these little things feel like the only revolutionary work I have ever done.

255

"It's not too hard to work around kids?" my mother says in a gentle voice that is almost the only thing she can still do to make me tense with anger. Forget that it's too late for some things: sympathetic hugs, motherly advice.

"No," I say. "Sometimes." I practise the belly breathing I read about in a book on forgiveness and it helps. Slow deep breaths into the abdomen.

A baby was what I really wanted.

We tried. Instead we had early blooms of unexpected blood and grief. And the two ectopic pregnancies, one for each tube. Those were little stones. My body's formed its own history of the Old Man's big silver ring, and of reckless nights after the revolution spent looking for something or someone to believe in. Those nights I spent drunk and high trying to drown out the memory of the Old Man's voice whispering *pretty little girl*, knowing he was a liar, and wishing again that he wasn't. The doctor said the causes for these things were hard to pinpoint but I knew that this was my red star tattoo, the scar to remember it all by.

I focus on the pattern of my breath, the expansion and contraction of my muscles. These new things that must be forgiven: Mortality. Frailty. The body itself.

By the next day my mother is feeling better. She shows me her newest work, wildlife prints and words stamped on her preacher father's old Bible. She says some people find them sacrilegious but she meant it just the opposite. A way to honour the spiritual. Her father never even wanted to become a preacher, that was just something that was expected, a job in his father's salvation business. He'd been a gambler and a cheat but he'd also been against the Vietnam War, a reader, a man who loved flowers. She gives me a print to take home. *In good we trust,* it reads.

Kevin and I get ready to go. We leave some cash to pay a dog walker. Just before we go my mother shows me a cardboard box.

"Here," she says. "I thought you might want to have this."

Inside are pages of my letters and writing and copies of my mother's letters to me, as well as ones she never sent. Letters, poems and essays going back to my early teens, the weight of the box proof of both the separation and connection we maintained during my childhood.

In almost every letter I'll find evidence of how we can remember and forget. The fine balance between knowing and not knowing that my childhood seemed to require. But first it will sit for weeks in a corner. I habituate myself to its dimensions, to its existence. And then I start to read.

The letter she wrote to me in Montreal not long after I left Redding.

257

When I think about you and wonder if I will ever get to be a mother again and when the emotions well and the tears start I just read what you wrote on the book you gave me, about revolutionaries shedding blood and not tears and I find something I need to do so I don't dwell on it.

The first letter she sent to me after I told her about Karl.
I knew.
The letter I sent back to her.
You knew why didn't you tell me.

"When you were little you could guess the suit of the cards before I even turned them over," my father said.

"You were a very loved baby," my mother told me. "But you were so slow to sit up we worried there was something wrong with you."

My sister said, "You just liked being taken care of."

From these stories came my own. That I knew. That I hung on to my dependence, to all the love and power my chubby baby fingers could hold. Because I knew it wasn't going to last forever.

I was a loved baby who was born into an interesting time. Bullshit, the Old Man said and like everything else about him that was part terrible truth and part terrible lie. In a year or two from now when I finally tell my family I'm going to publish a book my mother will write to me that she is "honored to be the mother of a writer." My sister will ask if there's anything she can do to help. And my father will call me and say, "If you have to choose between my feelings and the truth, pick the truth. Say whatever you have to say."

But on the Sunday as I carry the box out to the car all I know is that this moment is a page in the story, this history and its weight are a page in the book that I was always writing, a fairy tale, where I fell down a rabbit hole. Where I could be magic if only I learned how. The true history of the revolution. Or maybe only what I was sure happened. But it was always about people who wanted to be loved. Who wanted to be happy. And how hope made them both blind and free, one transforming into the other, like water to steam and back again. Smart and stupid, fearful and brave.

And when I write it all down will I say that my mother is clearing away the memories that fill up the small rooms where she needs to live, making way for the self, the self that not religion or motherhood, not communes or communists could contain? In that version I am—still—too small to compete with my mother's beliefs, but big enough to be in the way. Or will I say that my mother is not clearing out boxes but offering me pieces of the postmarked truth, evidence for the stories she knows I need to tell?

These are some of the things I think about on the drive home.

259

ACKNOWLEDGEMENTS

When you are writing the acknowledgements for a book about your life, are you thanking people for the book or the life? Both I guess.

To the hundreds of people in my childhood who talked to me like I had something to say, who gave me books or snacks or advice when it looked like I could use them, thank you. Some of you are friends, some of you I lived with in communes or field offices and some I met in moving cars or at parties or in meeting halls. If it takes a village to raise a child, thank you for being part of my village.

To the front-line cadre still inside the organization, thank you for caring about the poor, the disenfranchised, the exploited. I have never doubted your spirit of hope and justice. Maybe things are different now. Maybe you are free to speak up or walk out, to hold your leaders accountable. I hope for your sake that is true.

It goes without saying that you cannot write a family memoir without a fucked-up family and so I thank my family for the bad decisions that made for good stories and for the good intentions that made it bearable. I decided early on I could only speak for myself, for what I sensed, what I felt, what I understood at the time. That was hard enough. I am especially grateful to my family for understanding this. My mother who gave me the qualities that I admire both in myself and my sister—creativity and courage—and whose values I continue to honour in the work I do. My father who taught me that sometimes life isn't as complicated as it looks. That happiness can start with a really good meal, and Janice, who cooked us that meal. And for Patricia, my big sister whose big love has saved me more than once, and reminded me always that I was worth saving. Larsen twins forever!

Of course I am indebted to my friend, editor and Scrabble opponent Pamela Murray, who took a chance on me even without being blackmailed about our university years and whose insights have made my life and this book better. Many thanks also to Barbara Pulling, for both her editorial advice and her introduction to Trena White of the Transatlantic Agency, who has been such an advocate for my work. I am also deeply appreciative of the writing community I have met in the years I spent working on this book. To Joan Flood who said, "That's just your fear talking," when I started to doubt myself and to the many people who reminded me to be generous with myself and others, to work hard, to develop good habits, to be honest. To be brave. The things you sometimes need to be reminded of not only to write but to live.

And finally to Kevin, who I have loved possibly from the moment I held his hand and who has been there to hold my hand through every page. You are my special friend.

Sonja Larsen has written articles for magazines, short stories and poetry for literary journals, and term papers for rich, lazy students. She is a graduate of the Simon Fraser University Writer's Studio and her work has been published in the *Globe and Mail*, *Room*, and *Descant*, as well as a number of other print and online literary magazines. She works with youth in Vancouver's Downtown Eastside.